I LOVED HER IN THE MOVIES

Also by Robert J. Wagner

You Must Remember This (with Scott Eyman)

Pieces of My Heart (with Scott Eyman)

I LOVED HER
IN THE MOVIES

*Memories
of Hollywood's
Legendary Actresses*

ROBERT J. WAGNER

WITH SCOTT EYMAN

VIKING

VIKING
An imprint of Penguin Random House LLC
375 Hudson Street
New York, New York 10014
penguin.com

PHOTOGRAPH CREDITS
Page 7: Collection of Robert J. Wagner
37, 53, 63, 69, 72, 92, 103, 109, 116, 119, 125, 138, 170, 184:
Collection of Scott Eyman
133: Film Favorites / Moviepix / Getty Images
135, 221: Silver Screen Collection / Moviepix / Getty Images
147: The Bruce Torrence Hollywood Photograph Collection
165: Michael Ochs Archives / Moviepix / Getty Images
197, 213: ABC via Getty Images
203: Michael Ochs Archives / Getty Images
208: Ron Galella Collection / Getty Images
217: Time & Life Pictures / The Life Picture Collection / Getty Images
229: John Downing / Hulton Archive / Getty Images

Library of Congress Cataloging-in-Publication Data

Names: Wagner, Robert, 1930– author. | Eyman, Scott, 1951– author.
Title: I loved her in the movies : memories of Hollywood's legendary actresses /
Robert Wagner with Scott Eyman.
Description: New York : Viking, 2016.
Identifiers: LCCN 2016041551 (print) | LCCN 2016042365 (ebook) |
ISBN 9780525429111 (hardback) | ISBN 9780698195868 (ebook)
Subjects: LCSH: Wagner, Robert, 1930– | Actors—United States—Biography. |
Actresses—United States—Biography. | Actresses—United States—Anecdotes. |
BISAC: BIOGRAPHY & AUTOBIOGRAPHY / Personal Memoirs. |
BIOGRAPHY & AUTOBIOGRAPHY / Entertainment & Performing Arts. |
BIOGRAPHY & AUTOBIOGRAPHY / Rich & Famous.
Classification: LCC PN2287.W235 A3 2016 (print) | LCC PN2287.W235 (ebook) |
DDC 791.4302/8092 [B]—dc23
LC record available at https://lccn.loc.gov/2016041551

Printed in the United States of America
3   5   7   9   10   8   6   4

Set in Fournier MT Pro
Designed by Francesca Belanger

For the women I love:

My daughters Katie, Natasha, and Courtney.

My sister, Mary.

And for Jill—my wife, my love, my best friend.

You have all brought me so much happiness and joy.

CONTENTS

I LOVED HER IN THE MOVIES

INTRODUCTION

The great choreographer George Balanchine famously said that "Ballet is woman."

"It is easier to make dances for men," he said. "They jump, they turn. A woman is more complicated . . ." Another time he compared women to orchids: "You have to know exactly how much sun, how much water, how much air and then take them inside before they wilt."

He was, of course, right, but I'd go further. To my mind, there's something profoundly feminine not only about ballet but about the movies as well. Not just because sexual attraction is often the magnet that pulls us to one movie star and not another, but because there's something in the nature of the moviegoing experience itself that approximates the reverie that overtakes you when you're in love with a beautiful woman. Going to the movies drops you into a neutral dream state, in which you first become receptive, then, hopefully, enchanted.

Think about it. We step into the darkness, where we let go of whatever it is that's been bothering us. We relax. The screen comes alive, and we focus on something outside ourselves—the plot, the characters. We become willing prisoners. Unless the filmmakers are inept, we don't question, we just accept what we see in front of us. As with love, reality has little to do with the experience—things can happen faster than they would in real life, or much, much slower, but we suspend more than our disbelief. We suspend the various negative states we dragged into the theater.

Despite the expanding shores of television and all the great work being done in that medium, it can't duplicate the thrill of seeing movies in a theater. When you're watching TV, you're sitting in the living room, the lights are on, the kids or grandkids are running around, the dog hears something outside and begins barking, and if you're not absolutely riveted, you might check your e-mails. TV lacks magic, but movies always contain, at the very least, the possibility of enchantment.

Just as in dreams, sometimes there's an erotic component in films that can be startlingly intense. They say that the most important years in defining your tastes in the opposite sex are from about seven to fourteen or fifteen. I have to agree—the sight of Maureen O'Sullivan in her artfully arranged rags in MGM's Tarzan pictures provided a source of never-ending excitement for this particular adolescent.

All this is why I've written this book about the female movie stars who defined my generation as well as succeeding ones—it's about what binds Kay Francis to Marilyn Monroe, what connects Bette Davis with Glenn Close . . . as well as what separates them.

As a young boy growing up in Westwood, I watched many of these women from the remove of a center-row seat at the Fox Theater. As I grew older, my luck increased exponentially—I got to work with many of them, and know many more. I've worked with about half of the legendary leading ladies of my lifetime: from Bette Davis and Marilyn Monroe and Barbara Stanwyck to Audrey Hepburn, Elizabeth Taylor, and Sophia Loren.

And Natalie.

Not to mention Janet Leigh, Joan Collins, Joanne Woodward, Debbie Reynolds, Capucine, Jennifer Jones, Stefanie Powers, Angie Dickinson—and a certain Jill St. John, with whom I not only acted but married.

Then there were those I knew socially: Gloria Swanson, Lana Turner, Joan Crawford, Gene Tierney, Loretta Young, and dozens of others.

I may as well admit to at least one basic prejudice: I think women in general have it tougher than men, and I think actresses in particular have it tougher than actors. On the other hand, they're better equipped to cope than men are because women are more realistic. Not stronger necessarily, but more self-aware. And, in a strange way, less vain. Actors—and I don't except myself—can walk around in a semiblissful state, their innate masculine vanity preceding them into the room by a good five yards. If they're successful actors, they can be much worse. Actresses may use a lot more makeup, but that means they have to be cognizant of their weak points and strong points, and how best to disguise that which needs to be disguised.

I've spent more than sixty-five years in show business and I've given actresses a lot of attention and a lot of thought. So this is a book about the species "Actress" as I knew it, and the similar and unique characteristics of these remarkable women. I'm going to consider not only what they were like on screen and off, but also why they became stars, and how their specific emotional and dramatic chemistries affected the choices they made as actresses, as well as the choices they made as women. I'll also discuss the strange alchemy of the camera—how it can transform the attractive into the stunning . . . and vice versa.

One point I want to make clear up front: There is little badmouthing of the women I write about here. This is not because the movie business is free of difficult people; on the contrary, it's full of them. (A few will be mentioned, but they won't be dwelt on.) Producers will shaft you, directors have their own agenda that may or may not agree with yours, and they'll all do what they need to do to get what they want. And don't even get me started on the bureaucrats who run movie studios today.

But I respect the acting profession and most of the people in it. Very few actors will sabotage their colleagues. I can count the number of professionally duplicitous performers I've worked with on one hand. For one thing, you need other actors if you're going to be any good. Acting is really reciprocal self-interest—when it's good it's like a competitive tennis match in that the better the people you're playing with are, the better you'll be, though it's better than any tennis match because nobody loses. Which is why an actor will almost never shaft another actor. Not only is it bad karma, but that other actor is often your only friend in the world in that acting moment, as it's taking place. It's just the two of you, and nobody knows what happens then quite like another actor.

I met and worked with these women from the middle of the twentieth century to the present, but for the sake of organization I generally discuss each of the actresses in the decade in which she became famous, which will enable me to compare different generations of talent, and to highlight how acting and standards of beauty have evolved over time.

This is a book about character and craft, talent and genius, respect and love, and how those qualities united to form some of the most legendary careers in the history of a great art form. At times it may sound like a love letter, and I guess it is—a love letter to actresses.

THE THIRTIES

When I was a little boy, I had a treasure chest. The Gospel of St. Matthew says that where your "treasure" is, so is your heart, which completely describes how much the contents of my chest meant to me when I was eight years old.

It was slightly larger than a shoebox, perhaps five or six inches high and made out of cedar, so it had that great smell that always seems to derive from something finer than mere wood.

My chest contained the things that meant the most to me. There were the letters and postcards that my mother wrote me when I was at boarding school, a place I loathed as a child and, three quarters of a century later, still do. There were also cap guns, matchbooks, and a picture of Dick Tracy, the comic-strip hero who was the idol of kids everywhere, mostly because he had such wonderful toys—a secret decoder ring, a watch with a two-way radio in it. (Nobody could devise grotesque villains like Chester Gould, and kids love the grotesque.)

I also had a picture of William Boyd as Hopalong Cassidy atop his horse Topper, who I thought was the most beautiful horse in the movies, so much so that I would name my own horse after him. Topper starred in at least fifty movies with Boyd, and though my horse Gray Topper made only one movie, it was a good one: *Louisiana Purchase* with Bob Hope.

Years later, it would be one of the thrills of my life to meet Bill Boyd, who turned out to be a terrific man with a gorgeous wife named Grace Bradley, who had fallen in love with him when she was a little girl watching the silent pictures Bill had made for Cecil B. DeMille. A

dozen years later, she made her way to Hollywood and started working at Paramount, where she met Bill, married him, and lived happily
ever after.

By all rights, my autographed picture of Norma Shearer should
have been in my treasure chest, but it was too big; I kept it in a special
folder. Norma Shearer was the first movie star I ever met. The year was
1938, I was eight years old, and I was going to school with her son,
Irving Thalberg Jr., at the Hollywood Military Academy on San
Vicente Boulevard, where our parents had sent us because . . . well,
actually, I've never been quite sure why they sent us there.

Neither Irving nor I could have been considered discipline problems. It's entirely possible that we were enrolled there because that's
where a good percentage of parents in Beverly Hills and Bel-Air educated their children—groupthink. Perhaps there was some kind of status attached to having a kid at the military school.

Anyway, I boarded at the school, while Irving went home every
day to Santa Monica. On weekends, boarders' friends would invite
them to spend the weekend with their families. Irving was a nice kid
who struck me as somewhat shy, although in retrospect it might very
well have been anxiety over his father's death from pneumonia two
years earlier.

Norma Shearer had spent eighteen months after Thalberg's passing off the screen, working through her grief and bargaining with
MGM over her late husband's stock holdings. She won those negotia-
tions, but Norma had a way of winning. And then it was time to go
back to work.

What made my first meeting with her so curious was that I had never
seen Norma in a movie at that point. For that matter, I wasn't even aware
that she was a movie star. All I knew was that she was Irving's mother.

The Thalberg-Shearer house was a French-Normandy confection
right on the beach. You walked into a courtyard that was filled with
flowers, through the front door, and up a set of stairs. The colors tended
toward the neutral, which was the style in that era—Irving Jr.'s room

Norma Shearer

was decorated in a sort of rose, blue, and ivory. The only thing that struck me as odd were framed photographs of his parents hanging on his bedroom wall, just in case he ever forgot who they were.

I was in my school uniform, all polished buttons and shined shoes. A butler took us up to Norma's room, while I gaped at the surroundings. Irving had told me his mother was making a film called *Marie Antoinette*, but that was meaningless to me because I didn't know who Marie Antoinette was. The décor struck me as ornate by the standards of our own Spanish-style home, so I was convinced that I was in Marie Antoinette's house. This conviction turned out to be very confusing; when I finally saw the film, I expected to see the house I'd been in, but didn't recognize any of it.

The butler showed us into her bedroom, which didn't surprise me, because I had already gotten the distinct feeling from Irving that his mother spent a great deal of time there.

Norma was sitting up in bed, and couldn't have been more gracious. She didn't have the ethereal glow that would strike me when I saw her in the movies, but then William Daniels hadn't lit her bedroom.

She asked about my parents and then about the classes I took with Irving Jr. Even though I was just a kid, the atmosphere was swankier and more complicated than just meeting the mother of a classmate; it was more like an audience with a queen.

The room was a shade of blue that was new to me; it was only years later that I realized it was delft blue, with some chartreuse and white accents. Although the Pacific Ocean was only a hundred feet away, you couldn't hear a thing—the walls must have been three feet thick.

Norma sent me away with a still autographed to "To Wagner." I'm not ashamed to admit that I still have it. I was in her presence for perhaps ten minutes, and I've never forgotten that visit.

I'm sure Norma Shearer wouldn't have remembered our meeting if I hadn't gotten to know her fifteen or so years later and reminded her of it. For her, it was just a momentary duty that was a function of her identity as a mother. But for me, it was a mini earthquake.

I had met Norma Shearer! I hadn't known she was special before we met, but I knew she was special as soon as I walked into the room, and that impression was only reinforced whenever I told people I had met Irving's mom. The general response was along the lines of "You met Norma Shearer? *She's a movie star!*"

How many other kids at the Hollywood Military Academy could make that claim? For that matter, how many other kids in the *world* could make that claim? I had learned in the best way possible that movie stars had a dual existence: They appeared on the silver screen, but they also existed offscreen as actual human beings, and millions of people have spent a great deal of their time trying to assimilate the two apparently mutually exclusive halves of that equation.

At the time of our brief meeting, Norma's professional judgment was getting a little shaky. *Marie Antoinette* was wildly expensive; even though it attracted large audiences, it cost too much to show a profit. After that, she made *The Women*, which was a success. She had vague longings to play Scarlett O'Hara but wasn't seriously considered for the part, and then she turned down *Mrs. Miniver* because she didn't want to play the mother of a grown daughter. Instead, she opted to star in a pair of weak romantic comedies that both flopped.

So it was that only a few years after we met, Norma Shearer decided to walk away from the movies. She was forty-two years old. It was a strangely subdued exit for a woman who had ruled MGM.

Norma was born in a Montreal suburb, a determined little girl without a lot of the natural attributes that might have indicated a career in the movies. She played the piano quite well, a skill she demonstrated in several films, and for a time she thought about a musical career. But her father made some bad investments, and the family had to sell the piano, which meant that Norma had to devise a Plan B.

She did some modeling, worked as an extra, and was getting some work in movies by 1922. Norma had a trim, brisk quality, kept her hair short and chic and her manner cheerful and upbeat. She had a lithe, lovely figure, but she also had a tight, thin mouth, and one eye wasn't quite plumb with the other. But as I've learned in a long career, if you have to choose between talent and determination, go for determination every time.

Norma wed Irving Thalberg in September 1928 and their marriage immediately vaulted her ahead of every other actress on the MGM lot, with the exception of Garbo.

Every really great star offers something familiar that an audience has come to expect in their favorite actors and actresses, but presents it in a new package. Leading ladies are going to be beautiful, men are going to be handsome, or at least striking, but there has to be a little something extra, something unique in the mix if they're going to succeed in the long term.

Contrary to those who argue that she wouldn't have been anything without Irving Thalberg cherry-picking projects for her, Norma had been a considerable star before they married, in such roles as a cheerful barmaid in Ernst Lubitsch's *The Student Prince in Old Heidelberg* and an ambitious young actress in *Upstage*.

What Thalberg did do for his wife was to raise her to the highest level of stardom by casting her in gilt-edged properties that had a high probability of success; he didn't make her a star, but he made her a much brighter star than she would have been on her own.

This doesn't disqualify Norma from critical consideration, because the path of her career is typical of most starring careers—they have to be managed. There are very few stars who are their own best managers, who can function on a self-contained basis. Garbo came close, but even then it was MGM that figured out a formula for her pictures that would be acceptable to mass audiences: She loved, not wisely but too well. And she suffered. Boy, how she suffered.

Whether the setting was the past (Garbo often worked in period films) or the present, no expense was spared when it came to her wardrobe and the settings. After about 1928, she was presented in one primary way—as a woman only recently awakened to sex, who finds herself capable of the most transformative love imaginable, love with a touch of the holy to it, love that often led to great sacrifice. She may have been a bad girl before, but true love turned her into an idealist.

That was how the studio persuaded the mass audience into accepting Garbo, despite the fact that she resembled them not at all, not physically—*nobody* has ever resembled Garbo physically—and certainly not emotionally. MGM made sure that Garbo gave up everything for love . . . or was willing to.

Garbo's primary attribute was her face, which was infinitely fascinating—you couldn't get enough of looking at it, and because her displays of emotion were always muted, the dramatic effect was quite subtle. You never really got tired of either her face or her acting.

But there was only one Garbo.*

Norma's great attribute, in contrast, was versatility: She could play sentimental dramas, romantic comedies, and out-and-out farce. She even tried Shakespeare and got out alive. She could play crude, but not convincingly. In the early 1930s, she played a series of women who discovered their sexuality by stepping out on their faithless husbands or boyfriends.

Norma had it both ways; although her strength, her fallback position, was always class (which is what she embodied in her own life), she was a harbinger of the modern woman in movies like *The Divorcee* and *Riptide*, where it was made quite obvious that she enjoyed what a man did to her in bed. "I'm glad I discovered there's more than one man in the world, while I'm young enough and they want me," she announces to her errant husband in *The Divorcee*. "From now on, you're the only man in the world my door is closed to!"

---

*I actually talked to Garbo once. Sydney Guilaroff was doing Natalie's hair on *Splendor in the Grass* when the phone rang. It was a woman who wanted to talk to Sydney.

"Who's calling?" I asked.

"Garbo," she snapped.

"Oh." I think my heart stopped. "Well, let me get him for you."

That was it. Robert Wagner, intimate of legends.

These pictures shook people up. "[Norma Shearer] has murdered the old-time Good Woman," intoned *Motion Picture* magazine in 1932. "She has cremated the myth that men will never marry 'that kind of woman.'"

The fact of the matter is that Norma wasn't doing anything that her public wasn't doing. One out of four women born between 1890 and 1900 had lost her virginity before marriage. For women born between 1910 and 1920, it was seven out of ten.

Norma even pretended to play the part of the libertine offscreen, although in fact she was a very faithful wife to Thalberg. In one interview she declared, "The morals of yesterday are no more. They are as dead as the day they were lived. Economic independence has put woman on the same footing as man. A discriminating man and a fastidious woman now amount to the same identical thing. There is no difference."

Culturally speaking, in 1932 those were fighting words everywhere except in certain plush precincts of major cities. In some places, they're still fighting words. But Norma was essentially right.

Norma's great flaw was a quality that grew more pronounced as she got a little older—her need for nobility. It shows up in everything from *Marie Antoinette* to *The Women*, which is one of the reasons that Joan Crawford steals the latter picture: Joan is letting go and having fun playing a frankly greedy female, while Norma is playing the loyal wife to the hilt. Lesson: A self-aware, charming villainess with a sense of humor is a lot more fun than a dutiful heroine sticking around for the sake of the children.

But it needs to be said that in the last part of *Marie Antoinette* Norma is remarkable. Something in her responded to the plight of a woman who is losing everything—her lover, her child, her position, her life. It was as if she sensed what was waiting for her just around the corner— she'd already had to face the death of her husband, and perhaps had a premonition about the end of her career.

Because of her kindness to a kid she didn't have to be kind to, I've always had a soft spot in my heart for Norma. I still do. I saw her regularly years later, usually at Sun Valley, where she liked to go skiing with her second husband, Martin Arrougé. Marti looked a great deal like Irving Thalberg, except he was extremely athletic, unlike Thalberg, who had been limited by the rheumatic heart that shortened his life. I respected Marti—he made Norma extremely happy, he was devoted to her, took impeccable care of her, was there for her every minute of the day. He sincerely loved her.

Socially, Norma always remained the star, making an entrance so that you never forgot for an instant who she was, and even if you didn't happen to know who she was, you could certainly tell that she was Somebody. Since I liked to study the radiant female of the species, Norma's affectations were attractive, but I could see how it would be difficult to live with someone like her. In fact, both of Norma's children, Irving Jr. and Katherine, kept their distance from their mother in later years. Irving became a professor of philosophy in Chicago, and Katherine ran a bookstore in Aspen. The Thalberg bent for quality came out in Katherine. Her bookstore, Explore, is one of the finest I've ever been in, created with loving hands, in everything from the furniture and shelves to the stock of books. In her own way, Katherine Thalberg was a kind of artist, as well.

As for Norma, later in her life she seldom ventured east of Sun Valley.

In our occasional conversations when she was older, she admitted that she had been a fiercely ambitious young woman, but she seemed perfectly happy in her retirement. Unlike other great stars who walked away from the movie business—Mary Pickford, Garbo—she never made any tentative moves to get back in the game.

It's fair to say that Norma's reputation today is not what it was at the height of her fame, mostly because of the type of woman she played and the kind of films she made later on in her career, which are the ones that most people now see. Well-dressed, loyal wives in sentimental domestic dramas are relics of an earlier time and that time's dramatic conventions. They can be watched now more as interesting sociology than as involving dramas.

But Norma Shearer was my first movie star. She began my habit of thinking about stars, how they lived, and why they flourished . . . or didn't. Her picture didn't fit in my treasure chest, but her memory has always had a special place in my mental equivalent. Norma Shearer happens to be on the top of the list because she was the first. But there are others from that era that I also cherish.

I was born in 1930, so I grew up following the stars of the period before and during World War II. I had no personal memory of silent films, although I began watching them years later, and I was enthralled. It wasn't just the delicacy and firmness of Lillian Gish; it was the way someone like Clara Bow could express complete freedom, or how Louise Brooks could embody sex without a trace of the guilt or sentimentality that infested the popular attitudes of the day. Every generation thinks it has invented sex, but the people who were growing up just before and after World War I really might have, at least insofar as America is concerned.

Of course, on-screen in that period, the biggest female movie star was Mary Pickford, who generally played girls ten or fifteen years younger than her actual age. But there are actors who serve as comforting anchors in changing times, and there are other actors who signify those changing times. Pickford was one of the former, Norma Talmadge and Gloria Swanson the latter. All of their careers were stunted or ended by sound.

There were a few women directors in the early days of the silent era—Alice Guy-Blaché, Lois Weber—but with the onset of sound, women were traditionally slotted into other jobs: screenwriting, certainly, and editing, frequently. Margaret Booth was a huge power behind the scenes at MGM, where she was supervising editor, and who was still at it in the 1970s, when she ran Ray Stark's editing operation.

Dorothy Arzner began her career at Paramount as an editor and ultimately worked her way up to the director's chair by the beginning of the sound era. By the end of the 1930s, when I started going to the movies, Arzner was the only woman director in the business. Arzner's ascendance occurred during a period in which movies themselves were changing, and not necessarily for the better. The Production Code, which was instituted in mid-1934, was the result of intense lobbying by predominantly Catholic pressure groups, among them Martin Quigley, who published a trade paper called *Exhibitors Herald*.

Quigley and others became convinced that the movies had to have a set of immovable standards. Since the industry has always been terrified of federally mandated censorship, which was being urged by William Randolph Hearst, they acquiesced to self-censorship, in spite of the wisdom of people like Irving Thalberg, who insisted that "The motion picture does not present the audience with tastes and manners and views and morals; it reflects those they already have."

The Production Code mandated, among many other things, that crime had to be punished; that the vaguest suggestion of sex, even between a husband and wife, was out of line; and that gory violence was verboten. The movies that flourished in the very early 1930s, before the enforcement of the code, were much bolder, and when you see them now on Turner Classic Movies, they're frankly amazing— blunt, sometimes coarse. In *Baby Face*, Barbara Stanwyck climbs the corporate ladder by sleeping her way to the top. These were films in which women took lovers, had babies, and dumped their husbands— sometimes in that order.

This period has recently become fetishized by some modern fans. In retrospect, while I like these movies, they don't move me the way the films of the 1940s do. It seems to me that they're more slice-of-life journalistic than they are sweepingly dramatic, and they lack the sumptuous power of the movies I grew up on.

But whether they were made before 1934 or after, one thing remained the same—women dominated the box office. The biggest stars tended to be women, and it was women who were reflexively featured on the covers of the dozens of monthly movie magazines that crowded the newsstands. Not every great female star of that era was an adult, however. There was, for instance, Shirley Temple, who just happened to be the second movie star I met.

That encounter wasn't really a big deal, and I mention it here only for the sake of completeness. My orthodontist was a man named Alfred Higson. I was nine or ten years old and sitting in his waiting room one day with my mother. There, across the room from me, accompanied by her own mother, was Shirley. I was startled, because Los Angeles wasn't New York, where you can walk down the street and see all sorts of famous people. Our mothers introduced us, we said hello, we were both polite and slightly awkward with each other, and that was the end of that—for the time being.

A few years later, I actually got to know Shirley. We often saw each other at the Bel-Air Country Club, where our parents were members. She was dating a friend of mine named Dare Harris, who later achieved fame under the name John Derek, and I tagged along on several of their dates.

Shirley was crazy about Dare, but then everybody was. Without question, he was the handsomest young man I've ever seen in my life— he stopped traffic. Dare was very generous to me, treating me like a younger brother, and took me with him everywhere he went. In later years, he became a curmudgeon, very demanding and egotistical, but as a young man he had a charming personality.

Shirley was a sweet, vivacious girl. She was sincerely interested in other people and wanted to hear about what was going on in your life. I carefully watched how she handled herself in public, and I realized that being Shirley Temple wasn't easy. She had been subjected to kidnapping threats since she was a small child, and she usually went out with a hat pulled low so the brim would cover her face. Being famous took away Shirley's freedom.

There must have been times when she wondered if it was worth it.

Shirley had the strangest career—a huge star at six, washed up by puberty. Well, maybe it wasn't that strange; the same thing happened to Jackie Coogan in the silent era and would happen to several other child stars, who tend to be famous only so long as they're cute. Mickey Rooney is one of the few who was able to sustain a career, though he had at least as many craters as peaks along the way.

A number of very talented, gifted people applied themselves to the problem of reconstituting Shirley's stardom when she became a young woman. Darryl Zanuck let her go after the expensive flop of *The Blue Bird*, and she went on to make movies for David O. Selznick, MGM, and John Ford, who had liked her when she starred in his film of *Wee Willie Winkie*. Some of the pictures she made for these men were successful, notably Selznick's *Since You Went Away* and Ford's *Fort Apache*, but they were successful movies in which Shirley Temple happened to appear, not successful Shirley Temple movies.

Shirley basically walked away from show business when she got married for the second time in 1950, and proceeded to live a long and happy life spent successfully focusing on politics and her family.

Our loss. Her gain.

I was a teenager when I first met Gloria Swanson. The year was 1948, and she had just gotten the part of Norma Desmond in *Sunset Boulevard*. I was going out with her daughter Michelle at the time, and I had just broken into the movies at MGM, making a tiny appearance in a movie directed by William Wellman called *The Happy Years*. (It shows up on Turner Classic Movies from time to time; if you watch it, you'll see me in what seems to have been my prenatal state.)

At the time, my knowledge of Gloria Swanson was limited. I knew she had been in silent movies, but in my mind she was mostly just Michelle's mother. Of course, my respect for her increased exponentially when I saw *Sunset Boulevard* a little more than a year later. Around Hollywood, it was regarded as the most glorious comeback in a generation, which didn't stop them from giving the Oscar to Judy Holliday, who was brilliant but had also played her part in *Born Yesterday* hundreds of times on stage.

Gloria's Norma Desmond was completely original and utterly unforgettable, and what made it all the more surprising was its emotional accuracy. In 1949, silent movies had only been gone for twenty or so years, but outside of the Silent Movie Theatre on Fairfax in Los Angeles, or the Museum of Modern Art in New York, they were regarded as antiques and more or less impossible to see. But now we're fortunate in that many of these films are available on DVD and Blu-ray, not to mention on Turner Classic Movies.

In one sense, Norma Desmond provided a confirmation of popular taste—silent movies must have been pretty grotesque if people like that became household names. To which I say, you should have observed some of the players in 1949 Hollywood.

Before *Sunset Boulevard*, Gloria's movie career had more or less ended in the mid-1930s. She had been the biggest female star of the 1920s, then made a terrible mistake by falling under Joe Kennedy's influence, as well as under Joe Kennedy. He convinced her that she should produce her own pictures for United Artists, but Gloria was an actress, not a producer. She couldn't control her costs, and everything she made went over budget. *Queen Kelly*, a movie written and directed by Erich von Stroheim, was never properly finished and resulted in a dead loss of $800,000, which was just about all her ready cash.

Along came talkies, and she had a big hit with her first sound film, *The Trespasser*, which seemed to put her back on top. But it was a fluke; audiences just wanted to hear what she sounded like. Curiosity satisfied, they moved on to other, younger talents. Each succeeding Swanson film made less money than the one before it; at one point, she had to sell her United Artists stock back to the company to raise the cash to finish a picture.

Irving Thalberg threw her a lifeline at MGM, planning to cast her in *Dark Victory*. When Thalberg died before that could happen, MGM

Gloria Swanson

sold the property to Warner Bros., where Bette Davis had a huge hit with it. Gloria never made a movie at MGM.

Sunset Boulevard changed everything, although not in terms of cash—Paramount paid her less than $75,000, a piddling amount of money for the starring part in a major feature, but the hard reality was that there wasn't a lot of demand for Gloria's services by then. The movie upped her recognizability to such an extent that she was able to leverage the picture into a continual buzz of activity for the rest of her life. Not much of that activity consisted of acting, but Gloria didn't seem to mind.

Gloria was generous. She knew I wanted to be an actor. *Everybody* knew I wanted to be an actor, because I broadcast my ambition to anyone who would listen, and quite a few who wouldn't. Gloria did her best to help me, giving Michelle and me copies of the script of *Sunset Boulevard* and putting us through our paces with Billy Wilder and Charlie Brackett's dialogue. I took William Holden's part, and Michelle played Nancy Olsen's.

Gloria was . . . *incisive*. There was never any doubt regarding what she thought about any subject. If you didn't ask her, she'd tell you anyway. She was always busy, always industrious. She had no bitterness about her faded stardom, about the lost fortune. She was not one to blame other people; I remember her telling us, "The acting life is difficult and if you don't have the stomach for it, do something else." Gloria gave me the impression that she had always expected to work for a living and that those expectations had been met. When I knew her, she was designing women's clothes and thoroughly enjoying herself. In my memory, Gloria is always en route from one place to another, one commitment to another. She had loved being a huge movie star, but she wasn't confined by it as so many great stars are; she had done it, she had processed its meaning, and she had moved on.

Because she had been in the movies since she was a teenager, and a very big star from about the age of twenty, she hadn't had a conventional progress into maturity. She had little formal education—she once told me that she hadn't even graduated from high school—but she was naturally inquisitive, always hungry for knowledge. There were always dozens of books strewn around her house.

The flip side to her natural curiosity was that she was prone to fads, some of which were more meaningful than others. When I knew her, she was already on the health kick that would occupy her for the rest of her life. Our modern interest in free-range food and vegetables that haven't been sprayed with chemicals would have brought an approving nod from Gloria, as well as a smug "I told you so!"

Gloria had the aura of a true star, which didn't mean she didn't have a sense of humor. She was tiny, barely five feet, and usually called attention to her size immediately, to defuse any disappointment on the part of the people who had just met her.

Although the character of Norma Desmond drew on some aspects of her personality—Gloria could certainly be imperious—others were inventions of the screenwriters. Like Norma, she adored Cecil B. DeMille, who had made her a star in a series of extremely entertaining marital comedies in the period after World War I. While she was giving Michelle and me direction in our scenes, she would keep up a steady stream of suggestions and reminiscences, just like a director in the silent days. She would talk about how the hardest thing to do in show business is comedy, unless it was playing a nominal character in a straight drama. "Anybody can be a character actress," she would say, "because there's usually something to seize on and play. A perfectly normal woman is the hardest—you have no props, you have only a thin character."

She went on to explain that Norma Desmond was far from a normal woman, that she had a dozen fascinating eccentricities and cowed nearly everyone she knew. A woman like that, she would say, is easy to play. The role was all pretense and mannerisms, so there was very little of the real Gloria Swanson to be found in it, and she seemed to like it that way. If an acting part came along, or even a part playing herself, she'd do it and be happy to do it, but she wasn't always scanning the horizon for the next acting job. She found the present every bit as interesting as the past, although she did think that the movies had deteriorated. She would also allow as to how it might just seem that way because the great days of discovery in the art of film—the time when everybody was figuring out how to photograph scenes to the best effect, how to act for the camera as opposed to the stage—were now firmly in the past. The innovations that had taken place since then were primarily cosmetic—first sound, then color, then widescreen—but the stories hadn't really changed all that much.

Now, of course, the stories are quite different, but I somehow think Gloria wouldn't be terribly impressed by them, either. She was very concerned with quality, and interested in scripts about human beings and emotional interactions, and there aren't a lot of those around these days.

The upshot of my time with Michelle and her mother: Gloria kept going, wrote a juicy memoir, and died at the age of eighty-six with her sixth husband in tow. Growing up with Gloria Swanson as your mother couldn't have been easy, and Michelle didn't become an actress but opted for a more conventional life. I cherish our time together, for it enabled me to get to know her mother—Glorious Gloria, who more than lived up to her name.

It seems to me now that if you were interested in women, the 1930s and 1940s were the richest time for movies in our history. The female stars came in all shapes and sizes and every imaginable emotional frequency.

To take just the top of the list: Greta Garbo, Marlene Dietrich, Katharine Hepburn, Irene Dunne, Claudette Colbert, Joan Crawford, Kay Francis, Bette Davis, Barbara Stanwyck, Carole Lombard, Myrna Loy, and Jean Harlow.

I could go on, but you get the idea. I didn't know them all, but I knew most of them. These were women with different personalities, different strengths and weaknesses, even different body types. In varying degrees, they are all remembered today.

Then there were actresses whose fame was more fleeting, like Deanna Durbin or Jean Arthur. You've got to be a pretty dyed-in-the-wool fan of old movies to have much of an image of them.

In both cases, the reason was that the women either couldn't or wouldn't deal with Hollywood any longer. They both simply walked away from the movie business at early ages.

Jean Arthur was a particular loss. She was an attractive but not knockout blonde with a gorgeous scratchy voice. She made some great movies with high-end talent: *Cameo Kirby* and *The Whole Town's Talking* for John Ford; *Only Angels Have Wings* for Howard Hawks; *The Plainsman* for DeMille; *Mr. Deeds Goes to Town*, *You Can't Take It with You*, and *Mr. Smith Goes to Washington* for Frank Capra; *A Foreign Affair* for Billy Wilder; and *The Talk of the Town* and *The More the Merrier* for George Stevens.

Stevens cast her in her last film, *Shane*, in a part that offered her nothing special. But Stevens understood that a strong actress can elevate an ordinary part, not to mention an entire movie.

Using only her voice, Arthur brought shadings that weren't in the script—a sense of regret and loss. This woman knows that Shane loves her; if the circumstances were different, she would allow herself to feel the same way.

Arthur worked for the best directors in the American film industry, and they all loved her. But Jean Arthur didn't share their enthusiasm for Jean Arthur. She had a terrible shyness and a sort of congenital unhappiness that got worse as she aged and grew more sensitive about that aging. Hedda Hopper called her "the least popular woman in Hollywood." *In print*. Today she'd probably be diagnosed as clinically depressed. She was simply insecure about her place in the world of the movies, and the fact that she was working in a business that subsisted on the most stunning women in the world could only have increased her sense of herself as a Plain Jane.

Jean Arthur

She left Hollywood in 1945 to play Billie Dawn in Garson Kanin's *Born Yesterday*, but left the play before it came to New York. She made it to opening night in the title role of *Peter Pan*, a part she had wanted to play for most of her life, but began missing performances and eventually left the show.

The rest of her life was a stop-and-start series of parts undertaken then dropped, and missed opportunities. She became a recluse in Carmel and concentrated on her animals. (Animals are a convenient object of affection for people who have been terribly disappointed by human beings. People break your heart all the time; animals only do it once—when they die.)

There was room in Hollywood for one-off actresses like Jean Arthur, because the movie industry catered to a wide audience and as a result made a lot of movies. Each studio turned out between thirty to fifty a year, plus various live-action shorts and cartoons, so they were hungry for talent, all kinds of talent. No possibility was overlooked.

Ray Bolger, the dancing genius who played the Scarecrow in *The Wizard of Oz*, was bigger on the stage than he was on film, and he made only a handful of movies. Because of *Oz*, though, people still know who Ray Bolger was. "The thing that astounded me," he once said, "was that they bought people. It was like you would go into a grocery store and say, 'Give me four comics and three toe dancers, and I want five girls and five male singers. I want nineteen character actors and I want some unique personalities.'"

If you made a cheesecake appearance on a calendar, if you could sing a little or did a radio show in Duluth, if you appeared on Broadway or on tour, if you won a beauty contest, chances are you'd get an appraisal from a movie talent scout. With any luck at all, you might even get a train ticket to Hollywood, with a screen test to follow.

The crucial thing to understand is that what Hollywood sold was not really the individual movie. The actual product being marketed was the star—the movie was merely the packaging. The vast majority of the people who were signed by the studios failed, not because they didn't have any talent, but because they didn't come across, didn't photograph effectively, didn't pop through the lens of the camera to imprint themselves on the frontal lobe of the viewer's brain.

Whether somebody photographs well is something you can never judge until they're actually before a camera. We all know people who close up in the presence of a lens, and we all know people who love to be in its gaze. I think it would be safe to say that the vast majority of the female stars were not only comfortable with the camera, they embraced it as if it were a new lover, which, in many cases, it was.

After the initial screen test, which captured more or less what a woman looked like when she walked through the studio door, the experts took over, deciding what had to be changed. What they were trying to do was, as Johnny Mercer used to sing, "Accentuate the positive, eliminate the negative."

Teeth would be capped, noses sculpted, hairlines changed, eyebrows shaped, a flat chest outfitted with curves. If a face lacked definition, a loss of ten pounds was sure to bring out the cheekbones. If a name was full of unpronounceable consonants, a new name would be ordered up—the only people who were allowed to keep ethnic names were supporting players: Maria Ouspenskaya, Joseph Calleia, Joseph Schildkraut, or Akim Tamiroff. And if a potential prospect seemed to have a requisite sparkle but was woeful at delivering dialogue, he or she would be handed to a drama coach.

When this process, which could easily take a year or more, was finally completed, young contract players were shoved in front of the cameras to sink or swim. If they seemed to have something, they were worked like rented mules, learning the trade the hard way: by doing it. To take just one example, Cary Grant made twenty-four movies between 1932 and 1936. When he started, he was a handsome but awkward young man. With time, he became the splendid construct known as Cary Grant. The studios learned how to showcase him, and he learned how to project his personality.

This process was especially fine-tuned for actresses, who often began their careers by being cast in small parts opposite leading men who were already successful. MGM's Andy Hardy series provided breakthrough exposure for young starlets as varied as Judy Garland, Donna Reed, Lana Turner, Kathryn Grayson, Ann Rutherford, and Esther Williams.

Since the vast majority of young talent was signed for short money, they were low-risk investments; the huge successes more than made up for the dozens who washed out. Not everyone was emotionally equipped for what amounted to the commodification of human beings on an industrial scale.

The upside was that because the studios made a wide variety of movies, from dramas to comedies to musicals to costume epics, actresses had access to a lot in the way of parts, which in turn meant that women in the audience had a lot more in the way of role models than the movies offer today.

Now, the window for female stardom has narrowed to a sliver, because the industry caters mostly to teenage boys, and men with the souls of teenage boys. Female leads are mostly Angelina Jolie and Sandra Bullock, followed by a passel of twentysomethings who all aspire to be the next Angelina or Sandra.

Superficially, the industry of earlier eras demarcated actresses by their sex appeal, or by their willingness to play suffering, but it went deeper than that. If the 1950s were the time of the teenager—and they were—the 1930s were the time of the adult.

Think about actresses like Myrna Loy or Irene Dunne, both of whom became hugely popular in the 1930s. They were movie stars, but they were also women you could relate to on a human level. Unlike Garbo, you didn't watch them from a distance.

Some studios were better at buying already-developed talent and showcasing it than they were at breaking out new personalities. When it came to developing stars, nobody did it better than MGM.

Take the case of a little girl named Lucille LeSueur, who was signed by the studio in 1924. She was eighteen, more or less, five foot three, a natural redhead, uneducated, and relatively inexperienced. She didn't have a lot, but then they weren't paying her a lot: seventy-five dollars a week to start.

But she had enough—mainly, an infectious personality and a huge drive to escape the poverty into which she had been born. That drive made her an actress who could be mightily convincing . . . *if* she was correctly cast.

Lucille was a tiny fish in what was already a large pond, so she did what she had to do to gain some leverage: She attached herself to a powerful older man named Harry Rapf, a producer at the studio. The story I heard was that she and Harry were in a restaurant, and she accidentally on purpose spilled a drink in his lap, and then helped him clean it up with great vigor and thoroughness.

The relationship with Rapf bought her enough time to learn how to project her personality on the studio's dime. She began to get small parts, then bigger parts, then starring parts. By then, she was not known as Lucille LeSueur, but as Joan Crawford.

And then she upped the ante by marrying Douglas Fairbanks Jr., a Hollywood crown prince. They weren't married long—four years—but by the time they divorced, Joan was set up, as both a star and a woman who could have any man she wanted.

By the time I started making movies, Doug Fairbanks Jr. was living in England, so we only met a few times. But he was always touchingly loyal to Joan and what they had shared. I asked him about her once, and he replied that she had been a very ambitious girl, but never mean spirited. "I only saw the agreeable side of her," he said.

Joan had drive. She also had a quality of directness I've always liked. She was never a particularly nuanced actress, but she was open to the camera in a very touching way. Men came and went with Joan, but her devotion to the camera never waned, because the camera was her true love. At her best, she had a great capacity for truth—when Joan was properly cast, she didn't seem to be acting, especially in her films of

Joan Crawford

the 1930s. She excelled at playing working-class women who were de-termined to get ahead, which is exactly what she was.

Like Stanwyck or Harlow, Joan was well suited to the audiences of the Depression. They all played women who didn't have anything going for them other than their looks and drive, but were determined to make their looks and drive sufficient. The alternative was unacceptable.

Joan and I had a brief, ships-in-the-night fling when I was a young man in Hollywood, and we saw each other occasionally at industry events after that. She was always gracious, in a *grande dame* sort of way. At the premiere of *Prince Valiant,* Joan came over to congratulate me. I was kneeling down to talk to her and the photographers were gathering to take our picture. "Stand up," she said under her breath. "I never look down at anybody!"

I loved Joan—she was *always* Joan.

As with Davis, as with Stanwyck, as with most of these women, work was their life, and when the work started to dry up, it became very difficult for them. They took the decline in their careers person-ally, and why shouldn't they? Once upon a time, they had been hired because they were young and vibrant and beautiful and talented, and now they weren't getting hired because they were no longer young or vibrant, and their beauty had transitioned to something else—with age came authority. The talent remained, but their brand wasn't in demand anymore.

For her part, Joan took what was available, which tended to be low-end suspense and horror pictures. She was quite good in *The Best of Everything* for Jerry Wald, but the film isn't well remembered. Her big late-life hit was *What Ever Happened to Baby Jane?*, a good picture with power and no small amount of compassion. Most of the pictures Joan made at the end of her career, though, were beneath her. Not that she cared—the fact that she was able to work was more important to her than the quality.

Although an actress like Bette Davis (or an actor like Vincent Price) could always launch themselves into the stratosphere and lend a touch of intentional camp humor to these kinds of movies, humor was never Joan's strong point—that would have been her drive, her need for respect, her earnestness. I think it was Scott Fitzgerald who said that if a scene called for Crawford to tell a lie, she'd give an approximation of Benedict Arnold selling West Point to the British.

New York intellectuals never had much use for Joan, even when she married Franchot Tone, who was one of them. It was, I think, a class issue. MGM wanted her to play lower-middle-class girls—the milieu she had practically killed herself to get out of. She took those parts until she grew to hate them. She wanted to be more than that; she wanted to play genteel, as she had willed herself to become off-screen.

Joan would always insist that it wasn't MGM that had made her a star but the public, and she was right. Irving Thalberg arranged for Norma Shearer to get adaptations of successful novels and plays that would be sure to get attention and respectful reviews. Joan never got that kind of treatment from the studio—the scripts for her films were comparatively minor. They derived their importance from the fact that she was in them, and because the audience took Joan as one of their own. She was the embodiment of their own dreams of success. Joan *mattered* to her fans, as they did to her.

She felt she owed her fans everything. If you wrote Joan Crawford a letter, you'd get a letter back, and not one written by a secretary, but one handwritten by her. Think about the dozens of hours every week she had to devote to answering fan mail. It explains so much about her, and it also explains why the audience felt such loyalty toward her.

When Joan went over to Warners in 1945, she made *Mildred Pierce*—the sort of movie that sums up not merely a career, but an entire studio, and beyond that, an entire genre: film noir.

Her main antagonist at Warners was, of course, Bette Davis, who had reigned unchallenged as the queen of the lot for over a decade. She now had competition, and Bette didn't like anything about Joan, whom she once snarlingly referred to as "that mannequin from Metro"—as if the studio's couturier Adrian had been responsible for her career. When a publicist brought the great portrait photographer George Hurrell to the studio to see if he could work his magic on Bette just as he had on Joan at MGM, Bette snapped, "I don't want to look like a piece of shiny wax fruit." When she arrived at the portrait studio, Bette instructed Hurrell to "Go easy on the glamour. I'm not the type."

For Bette, the goal was always to be an actress; if stardom was the result, fine. For Joan, the goal was stardom, and acting was the vehicle. If Joan heard the stories about Bette slagging her she never let on. She preferred to project a gracious noblesse oblige that she felt was becoming to a woman on the verge of middle age.

Even when she was playing a good wife, there was no question that Joan had a backbone of the strongest steel. Not only wouldn't she break, she wouldn't even bend very much—it was very hard for any actor playing opposite her to hold his own in their scenes together.

But look at how beautifully she worked with John Barrymore in *Grand Hotel,* or with John Garfield in *Humoresque,* two powerful but otherwise completely different types of actor. In both roles you believe Joan when she makes the transition from indifference or hostility to gradually opening up to her leading man. That was Joan's strength, and it made her abandoning herself to love in her films a moving experience.

I always had a lot of respect for Joan, because of where she'd started and because of her best work, which I would classify as some of her late silent pictures and a lot of her films in the 1930s on through *Mildred Pierce*. That's almost twenty years at the top of the game. And I had to respect the amount of effort she'd expended to get to where she was, and where she expected to stay.

Barbara Stanwyck could have played a lot of the parts Joan played, and that's a tribute to Joan's level of talent. But while Joan had a core of fatalism that I found interesting, there were also touches of self-pity in some of her performances. Barbara would reveal the anger and occasional bitterness that her impoverished early life had given her, but self-pity was alien to her.

Still, people dismiss Joan Crawford at their peril. She deserves far more respect than she gets.

There were a few actresses of this period that I never met, but whom I feel I knew nonetheless. Jean Harlow was all sunshine, very few shadows. Harlow was open and free. She wasn't particularly beautiful—her face had a pushed-in quality, like a Pekinese—but she had a spectacular body and she wasn't shy about displaying it. In her earliest films, she's amateurish, but she worked at it and got better fast. In *Dinner at Eight*, she holds her own with a bellowing Wallace Beery, the biggest ham in the business, and George Cukor gets a hilarious comic performance out of her. Victor Fleming wasn't in Cukor's class, but he did good work in *Red Dust*. In that performance it wasn't the director pulling her strings, but the essential Harlow coming through.

I think it was the warmth of Harlow's personality that made all the difference, that made the audience stick with her in the early years when she was learning how to act, how to react, how to read a line. She was so human. Harlow was the waitress at the diner, the good-hearted dame who would give her last dollar to a panhandler.

Harlow was like Mae West in that she made sex safe for the middle class because she was so unself-conscious about her display. You couldn't begin to fathom what sex with Garbo or Norma Shearer would be like—they were too remote. But sex with Harlow could be easily imagined, and undoubtedly was. Sex was something she obviously enjoyed, so the audience relaxed and enjoyed her.

Jean Harlow's early death at the age of twenty-six has to be regarded as a terrible loss, every bit as much as Marilyn Monroe's. In both cases, I think their best work was ahead of them, and it's fascinating to speculate on what parts Harlow would have played had she lived, and whether she would have been able to transition to other types of roles as she matured.

Mae West was entirely a creature of the 1930s, specifically the early 1930s, because after 1934, when the Production Code began to be heavily enforced, her screen character had to be bowdlerized. Until then she was a howl—a little, middle-aged pouter pigeon of a woman who wasn't particularly attractive but clearly thought she was, so everybody else played along. She was sexual and pleased about it, and intended to make the men in her life happy about it, too.

Nobody had ever seen an apparition like Mae West before her movie debut in 1932, and nobody's seen one like her since. She didn't play the courtship game, didn't pretend to be interested in matrimony as much as she was interested in a good roll in the hay. In any case, the latter was dead certain to precede the former.

Mae West had a long life and a long career, but her best work is contained in just two or three movies made before the censorship hammer came down.

Another of the gleefully irresponsible stars of the 1930s was Kay Francis. Tall, slender, and with a body made for the satin gowns of Travis Banton, Kay was not that old when she became a star, but her career was basically over within only ten years. While she could play the devoted wife and mother, as every actress had to at one time or another, she really came to life playing a glamorous, slinky, slightly footloose creature who did as she pleased, which reflected who she was as a woman.

Kay was invariably soigné, very classy and very sexy, in spite of a slight speech impediment that led her to pronounce "R" as "W." Her best work is probably Ernst Lubitsch's *Trouble in Paradise*, although commercially she hit her peak at Warners, with movies like *One Way Passage*, which once seen are never forgotten, at least partially because of Kay's unique quality of elegance shaded with resignation. Years later, I optioned *One Way Passage* for a remake. Roddy McDowall was going to produce, and Elizabeth Taylor was going to star in it with me. But the money wouldn't come; the studios regarded the story as archaic.

In talking about Kay Francis with people who knew her, it becomes

Kay Francis

clear that she didn't care all that much about acting—it was a way of establishing and maintaining a comfortable lifestyle that she enjoyed. When she got too old to headline movies at Warners, she produced a few pictures at Monogram, then simply retired. Kay had a life of great color and good times. Husbands came and went, as did lovers. She also had a good head on her shoulders—when she died in 1968, she left an estate of a cool million dollars to the ASPCA.

A woman after my own heart.

Cary Grant once told me that of all the women he worked with, Irene Dunne had the best timing. That took me aback—I had always thought Rosalind Russell was his best match when it came to comedy—but Cary was an absolute perfectionist in his work, and comedy is universally recognized as the hardest thing for actors to perform, so I have to defer to his judgment. (I would defer to *any* judgment of Cary Grant's.)

Irene's initial ambition was to be an opera singer, but her voice didn't have the necessary heft, so she downshifted to musicals. She was a leading lady for the Shuberts for years, then was cast in the 1929 touring company of *Show Boat*, which was her ticket to Hollywood.

She could play heavy drama, and she could also play screwball comedy. She did it not by playing the comedy as farce—Irene wasn't Carole Lombard, whose energy and willingness to be silly made her stand out. She could play farcical situations, but she acted them more as situation comedies—she played it as straight as possible. What gave it away was the twinkle in her eye.

Irene was probably always too mature to be considered overwhelmingly sexy. She was born in 1898, so she was either pushing hard on forty or past it when she had her biggest hits. She couldn't help but be conscious of this, so she was always very appreciative of a cameraman who made her look younger than she was.

She had a muscle in her chin that would tense up and cause a little line to appear, which in turn could create a small shadow on her chin in

Irene Dunne

close-ups. There was a sweetheart of a cameraman named George Folsey, who photographed my first film. (George went into the MGM cutting room and got some frames of my scene in *The Happy Years* and gave them to me. "This is your first close-up," he said. "There will be many more.")

George noticed her problem and decided to do something about it. He took a small spotlight, mounted it on a swivel, and put a dimmer switch on it. Whenever Irene was doing a close-up, Folsey would be sitting there very intently watching her, and when he saw the muscles in her chin start to tense up, he'd carefully turn on the dimmer switch, and the tiny amount of light shining on her chin would make the shadow disappear.

When Irene saw the rushes, she actually started to cry and thanked Folsey for getting rid of that little dark spot. That story indicates so much about the kind of pressure that the actresses of that time worked under, pressures that the public never knew anything about.

Irene was a serious Catholic, and there was never any doubt about her rectitude either personally or on-screen. She married Dr. Frank Griffin, a dentist, in 1928 and stayed married. She didn't do a lot of publicity, and she and her husband kept mostly to themselves, although they had a few friends who were likewise classy and dignified—Douglas Fairbanks Jr. and his wife, for example.

Irene had a lightness of spirit that, with the impeccable timing Cary Grant noted, made her a superb foil for him in both comedy (*The Awful Truth*) and drama (*Penny Serenade*). Cary's specific gift was that he made everybody who worked with him a little better than they were with anybody else. Other actors seemed a little sharper, a little more on point when they were teamed with him, but Irene might have come the closest to matching him moment for moment. And she had a quality of impish teasing that matched his own sense of fun.

In movies like *The Awful Truth*, Cary plays scenes condescendingly, as if Irene's character is a little dim. Not a good idea. Dunne had sincerity, but she also had irony, and she could put a man in his place subtly—just by raising an eyebrow. She once said an interesting thing about comedy: "The best way to be funny is to be cold-blooded and purely mental about it. It demands more timing, pace, shading, and subtlety of emphasis . . ." In other words, a raised eyebrow is better than running around slamming doors.

Today, Cary is revered, while Irene is . . . appreciated. I think the difference derives from the fact that Cary was so handsome, hence sexy, while Irene was never viewed as beautiful so much as attractive. You could imagine Irene as a friend or member of the family—your aunt or mother, hence her success as the title character in *I Remember Mama*. But Cary *glistened*; you could never imagine him as part of your life, which is why even other movie stars would do double takes when they saw him and get a little tongue tied.

If you look at Irene's career objectively, she had far greater range than most of her peers. She played in musicals and excelled, she played in comedy and excelled, and she played in dramas and excelled.

She worked so very hard to be natural; you never caught her acting, or even trying to be wacky in comic roles. And what I particularly appreciated was that she didn't do Oscar-bait parts—extreme characters, alcoholics or addicts, or stunt castings with heavy doses of makeup. (Well, she did do the latter, but only once, in *The Mudlark*, where she played Queen Victoria with a lot of rubber on her face.)

She played characters in the middle range, middle-class or upper-middle-class women with domestic problems, which meant that they were easy for the audience to relate to. People went to Bette Davis movies for a show—a dramatic rendering of highly dramatic characters in highly dramatic situations, very few of which would ever be experienced by the average woman on the street. People went to Irene Dunne's pictures to see their own emotional lives reflected back at them—quietly but firmly, and with impeccable taste.

Because of this sense of propriety, Irene got nominated for Academy Awards, five of them, but she never won. She should have, but that's the way of the world.

Although she may not have received the recognition she deserved, Irene took great care over the caliber of the films she made—she had director approval in her contracts and was very discerning about whom she would and would not work with. As a result, her batting average was quite high, and she knew it. She was loath to take parts that were second rate, or films for directors that were beneath the level of George Stevens or Leo McCarey. Other actresses would have hated her but for her own sense of modesty and proportion.

She segued to middle age so subtly that you didn't even notice it. *A Guy Named Joe* begat *Anna and the King of Siam* begat *Life with Father* which begat *I Remember Mama*. She made a few more films, then began scaling back, and did some work in TV. She turned down roles in notable films like *The Swan* and *Gigi* and seems to have quietly arrived at the decision that she had simply done enough acting. Irene lived modestly and held on to her money, so she didn't have to work.

Her career ended when she was in her midfifties by her own intent. She had no interest in trying to captivate younger audiences the way go-for-broke talents such as Bette Davis or Joan Crawford did, because she thought the thrillers and horror films they made at the tail end of their careers were unseemly.

What made her stand out for me was her quality as a woman. Irene was the sort of religious person who doesn't talk about her beliefs so much as live them, and it is that which has helped keep her name alive down to the present day. She was one of the major figures to support St. John's Hospital in Santa Monica, having personally raised over $20 million for it. Today the Irene Dunne Garden perpetuates her memory, as does the Irene Dunne Guild, a group of volunteers who provide assistance to patients.

Irene was so persuasive she could even get non-Catholics interested in the workings of the hospital. Jimmy Stewart was a Presbyterian from Pennsylvania, but Irene asked him to be on the St. John's board, and he complied with great enthusiasm. She managed to get MGM to donate a portion of the profits from the epic Western *How the West Was*

Won to it, and the huge roster of guest stars in the film worked for very little money and no percentages so as to maximize those profits.

Years later, Jimmy asked me to become a member of the Board of St. John's. I'm still on the board today, and happily so. Irene herself remained involved in recruiting sponsors and money for St. John's until very near the end of her own life in 1990, when she was ninety-two.

Irene and I had several conversations. I once asked her what her favorite film was, and she hemmed and hawed a bit before answering, "Oh, *Love Affair*, I suppose." I told her that she had surprised me; I would have thought she would have preferred *The Awful Truth* or *Show Boat*. She replied that she didn't like the movie version of *Show Boat*— she thought the play was better.

Another time she evinced a quiet pride in what she had accomplished. "Everything I did had a purpose," she said. "It wasn't just a superficial acting job for the moment. It was important to me. I always knew that acting was not everything there was."

Even the casual acquaintance I had with her revealed that Irene was the embodiment of a lady. Not a stuffy clubwoman, but a vibrant woman with humor and an interest in life. She was always very attentive to other people and their problems. For instance: There was a young publicist at Columbia named Bob Board who didn't like his job and was looking around for something else. He had a hobby of painting caricatures of movie stars on eggshells. Irene saw them and asked him to make some for her daughter, who lived across the street from me in Brentwood. Irene wrote Board a letter to thank him, and told him that if she could ever do anything for him, just let her know.

A few years passed, and Board was doing puppet shows for children. He wrote Irene to tell her about his new career, and she remembered him—her daughter still had the eggs with his caricatures on them. She called all her friends in Los Angeles, and for the next ten years, Bob Board made a good living doing puppet shows for the birthday parties of stars' children, not to mention the industrialists and non-show-business types who Irene tended to socialize with.

Bob Board always idolized Marian Davies, but Irene Dunne wasn't far behind, and you can see why. Even in old age, there was an elegance about her. She was one of those people who quietly set goals for themselves and then go about first meeting and then exceeding them. Her accomplishments in the world of show business were remarkable, but they pale next to her accomplishments as a human being.

The great Myrna Loy became known as "the perfect wife," a label that couldn't have thrilled her, as it implied a demon housekeeper who always has dinner on the table at 6 P.M. sharp. In fact, Myrna wed four times, so her marriage skills could reasonably be said to have ended at the studio gate. But on-screen, she worked seamlessly with actors as varied as Spencer Tracy, Cary Grant, Fredric March, Clark Gable, Ronald Colman, and Clifton Webb. Think about the different styles and varying rhythms of that group of actors, and think about the skill set it must have taken for Loy to mesh with each of them.

In her early days in silent films, Myrna was cast as sloe-eyed temptresses, but her voice and natural vivacity pushed her in a different direction once sound came in. In 1934, she appeared opposite William Powell in *The Thin Man*, and she was off on a hot streak, specializing in playing sassy women who expected to be in on whatever excitement the male lead was having.

Myrna and Bill Powell made marriage look like fun. Theirs was a completely modern relationship, and by "modern" I mean twenty-first century—a union of absolute equals. Powell's Nick Charles might have been a little too soused to project much sexual charge, but you believed that he and Myrna's Nora Charles really liked each other, so you believed in the marriage. While Nick drank, Nora sparkled and supported him. Nick might flirt with another woman, but only incidentally—only a fool would dump Myrna Loy.

When Tom Mankiewicz wrote *Hart to Hart*, I told him that I wanted the series to have some of the feeling I got when I watched the Thin

Man movies, right down to having a dog like the Charleses' Asta. Let me put it another way: *Hart to Hart* was creative plagiarism. When Tom had brought me the original script by Sidney Sheldon, it felt to me like a rip-off of the Matt Helm character that Dean Martin had been playing in films. I thought it was vulgar and I didn't want to do it. Tom and Mart Crowley turned it around so we could emulate something with class, as opposed to something crass.

Bill and Myrna made a lot of pictures together, and Loy had a starring career that lasted into the 1950s, which was very unusual for that time, largely because she could play both comedy and drama with charm and assurance.

The actresses of this period had a great deal of authority . . . assuming they cared to exercise it. Generally speaking, they were usually given veto power over their cameramen. Garbo insisted that William Daniels shoot her pictures, while Myrna was more concerned about directors than she was cinematographers. When Darryl Zanuck borrowed Myrna from MGM for *The Rains Came*, she insisted that Clarence Brown, her favorite director at MGM, make the picture.

This had all taken place twenty years before I heard the story, but Darryl still seemed miffed about it; the inference was that no Fox director was good enough to direct an MGM actress. Since Darryl had such talents as John Ford and Henry King under contract, this was clearly not the case, but what Myrna wanted, Myrna got.

So MGM lent out Brown, for the first and last time in his career at that studio, and he spent the rest of his life singing the praises of Darryl and the way he produced a movie. Brown always said that *The Rains Came* was the happiest picture he ever made.

Years later, when Myrna came back to Fox to make *Cheaper by the Dozen*, she was older and more docile, and accepted Darryl's choice in directors.

Myrna's comic specialty was unspoken disapproval. She could eye a man with a palpable air of disdain for the lovable lug. Her leverage was her unpretentious intelligence. She was the American woman par excellence, making up in insight and command what she lacked in physical size.

Claudette Colbert had similar gifts, but Claudette could carry a film by herself, as Myrna could not, perhaps because Claudette was more overtly sexy and might have appealed as much to men as to women.

Claudette could play anything—temptresses (*Cleopatra*), mothers (*Since You Went Away*), wives (*Skylark*). She could play screwball comedy (*It Happened One Night*), she could play heavy drama (*So Proudly We Hail*). Irrepressibly chic in the 1930s, she matured in the 1940s into something special; like Myrna Loy, but on a grander scale, she became the epitome of the American woman, as American women thought of themselves—witty, smart, resourceful, and incapable of giving up. Whatever fate dished out, Claudette could take it and look good doing so.

It was no secret that she was French and had come to America when she was a child, but nobody held that against her; Claudette Colbert was as intrinsically American as Joan Crawford, but much more elegant. She was only five or six when she arrived in New York, which accounted for her perfect English. Her original intent was to be a fashion designer, and to facilitate her drawing she attended the Art Students League across the street from Carnegie Hall in New York. She went into the theater more or less on a lark, and that segued into movies when she was only twenty-two, when she left New York and came to Hollywood as sound hit, along with a host of others: Barbara Stanwyck, Joan Blondell, Miriam Hopkins, and Bette Davis. Most of these women had a certain working-class quality, but not Claudette, who was always upper crust. A few years later, Kate Hepburn—speaking of upper crust—joined them.

I think Claudette's true gift might have been toward the lighter side of the scale. Even in a movie like DeMille's *Cleopatra*, which has a lot of the great showman's spectacular set pieces, Claudette conveys an irony that isn't necessarily present in the dialogue. She treats Henry

Wilcoxon's Marc Antony as if he's the cutest lummox she's come across in months. He may not be the sharpest sword in the armory, but he's cute. It gives the pairing a humor and strength that later, straighter interpretations of the part all lacked.

Claudette's reputation within the business was that of a cool, collected customer, very businesslike. I was a fan of hers at the time and became even more of a fan when I had the opportunity to work with her.

By the time I acted with her, Claudette had been a star for twenty years, and her status had never diminished. This was something of an amazing accomplishment, because Claudette didn't actually make a lot of great movies. *It Happened One Night,* certainly, and a few others. But most of the time she appeared in what can be classified as smooth entertainments.

It's easy to understand the career of an actress like Bette Davis— just look at her roster of memorable films. But Claudette mostly made very solid, professional movies, which is a guarantee of contemporary popularity, but not necessarily popularity with posterity.

Because acting had never been Claudette's primary ambition, she had a very levelheaded way of approaching it. For one thing, she understood the importance of projecting a consistent personality: She may have played all kinds of parts, but she tended to always look the same in them—wearing the same hairstyle and being shot consistently from the left side.

It was well known in the industry that she had had a car accident early on, and the bones in her nose had healed in such a way as to make the right side of her face look slightly different from the left. It wasn't anything out of a horror movie, but when the cameraman George Folsey—again!—told her that her right side was problematic, Claudette was convinced. After that, close-ups of the right side of her face simply didn't happen.

Around Hollywood, the right side of Claudette's face became known as "the dark side of the moon."

Claudette Colbert

Claudette observed this single rule with absolute fidelity. When George Hurrell wanted to shoot stills of her right side, Claudette shrugged and let him click away. But she made sure those shots never saw the light of day. I'm sure she had a conversation about how she would be photographed with directors of her films before shooting started.

I had always thought all this was an affectation until I happened to see one of her very early movies recently. It was made in 1931, before her dictates would be obeyed without question. Her left profile was, as always, symmetrical and perfect; her right was slightly off. I was forced to admit that Claudette, like the equally demanding Marlene Dietrich, knew exactly what was right for her.

The next time one of her movies from 1930 or 1931 runs, check it out. You'll find that George Folsey was right—the left side of her face *was* better. My favorite performance of Claudette's is in *It Happened One Night*, probably because she comes undone over the course of the movie. Claudette was always so collected, on screen and off, that I never believed she was capable of being ravaged or was likely to be. It was hard to imagine her discombobulated, although I certainly must have tried her patience on the film we made together.

I was twenty years old and appearing with Claudette in a movie called *Let's Make It Legal*. It was a young actor's worst nightmare. I was nervous and couldn't get the lines out, and the takes just kept mounting up. (I distinctly remember having to do forty-nine takes of a single scene.) Not all the errors were my fault, but most of them were. The day ground on, and my nervousness only increased. I was beyond green, and it showed. I didn't have much confidence to begin with, and I gradually lost what little I had.

Claudette's reaction? She hardly blinked, never evinced the least trace of impatience. I can only guess that something similar must have happened with her at an equivalent stage of her career, she had been met with patience, and she was paying it forward. Now, there are actors and actresses who get better the longer they work on a scene, but there aren't many. I was told that Garbo was good for maybe five or six takes and after that she got progressively worse. Kate Hepburn, on the other hand, was born to act, so she was perfectly content to go twenty takes or more if she thought there was any point to it. And Audrey Hepburn was a bear—she'd stay out there all day working on one scene.

But I got the distinct feeling that Claudette was closer to the five-or-six-takes-and-move-on school. She could easily have had me replaced by uttering a single sentence. Not only did she not have me replaced, not once did she roll her eyes, not once did she sigh, not once did she betray any impatience or anger at my incompetence.

It was an object lesson in the discipline necessary to be an actor, not to mention a star. On that nightmarish day, Claudette made no distinction between a distinguished veteran (her) and a fumbling rookie (me). The unspoken message was that we were an ensemble, a team, and if one of us was having a bad day it was up to the rest of the group to back him up. Every actor has a bad day at one time or another, but it happens to young, nervous actors most often, so they need the most support.

It's a lesson I've never forgotten and have always tried to impart on any picture or TV show I've done. It's an especially valuable lesson in TV, where a cast is working together as a group for years at a time, and directors come and go. The only constant is the actors, so esprit de corps is crucial. Claudette taught me that a true star stands by his or her co-workers and is there for them come what may.

On the set, these women were almost always pleasant pros, but you did have to be careful not to cross them, even accidentally. Shirley Temple told me about an experience she had had with Claudette during the filming of *Since You Went Away*. Shirley had been stealing scenes since she was four years old, so Claudette was on her guard. She was playing Claudette's daughter, and they had a lot of scenes together. During one take, Shirley moved so that Claudette had to turn around to follow her, whereupon her right side was about to come into view of the camera. It was classic upstaging.

"Claudette reached out and grabbed my chin," Shirley told me.

"She held on to my chin and rotated herself to a left exposure. She would not tolerate any tricks."

I don't know if Shirley's move was inadvertent or intentional. Nothing was said, but Claudette's meaning was clear.

I've always wondered how different *All About Eve* would have been with Claudette—who was originally cast as Margo Channing but bowed out shortly before shooting—instead of Bette Davis.

When Claudette threw out her back, Bette stepped in and revived her career. Claudette would have been good in the part—it's so well written that almost any actress outside of Marjorie Main would have been good in the part—but Bette brought something blazingly original to it, something that no other actress would have.

Bette delighted in showing the audience the raw places in the character of Margo. Would Claudette have been willing to do the same? Somehow I doubt it; I think she would have substituted irony for Bette's bitterness. The picture would still have worked—you couldn't kill that script with a cannon—but it would have lost some of its bite.

Claudette had a talent that only a few stars have: She managed her career brilliantly. She sustained professionally, and she had a sense of discretion about her private life. She was married to Dr. Joel Pressman, and the two of them were members of the Bel-Air Country Club, where I saw them frequently. He was an extremely pleasant man, somewhat asexual in manner and bearing. After he died in 1968, Claudette lived mostly in Barbados, where she adopted the lifestyle of Scarlett O'Hara, living in a lovely house manned by a platoon of black servants. Next door was the house of her female companion.

She was a movie star for more than thirty years, and when the parts in movies got uninteresting, she returned to the stage in comedies with leading men like Rex Harrison and Stewart Granger until she was eighty. Who else did that?

When I did A. R. Gurney's *Love Letters* on stage in London forty years after we had worked together, Claudette came backstage afterward to tell me I had been wonderful. I was just happy that she didn't mention that agonizing day on the set of *Let's Make It Legal*, but she was far too gracious to do that.

A great star. A great lady.

Sound brought a lot of interesting actresses to the movies, not all of whom are remembered today. Take Ruth Chatterton, who was born in 1893, which made her forty years old just about the time she was at her height. Chatterton was what was generally known as a handsome woman, but she had a powerful dramatic force, obvious in William Wyler's *Dodsworth*, in which she plays Walter Huston's vain, panicked wife. It's a great, brave performance, because Chatterton keeps her ego out of it; she never tries to win the audience's sympathy. You feel sorry for her because her character is so relentlessly deluded.

Offscreen, Chatterton was the same kind of woman as Kate Hepburn: She did as she damn well pleased. She flew her own plane, married three actors in succession—Ralph Forbes, George Brent, and Barry Thomson—and when she left the movie business, she wrote several successful novels.

Then there was Constance Bennett, who made a number of silent films, though not very successfully. But sound freed her up and showcased her very attractive, slightly husky voice. Her predominantly female audience responded to her in the same way they did to Bette Davis a few years later. For a time, Bennett was the highest paid leading lady in films.

Carole Lombard had also made silent films, but couldn't break out of the pack until sound revealed her great gift for comedy. Lombard was a fearless talent; she'd do anything, match herself against anybody— John Barrymore, Jimmy Stewart, or anybody in between.

All these women came to the movies as part of the vast reshuffling that rendered great silent stars like Mary Pickford, Norma Talmadge, Gloria Swanson, and Lillian Gish irrelevant. Pickford and Talmadge retired, Swanson kept busy until the staggering comeback of *Sunset*

Boulevard, and Gish reconstituted herself as a distinguished character actress equally at home on stage or screen.

Another actress of the same generation was Loretta Young, who was working on the Fox lot when I started there. She was always a great beauty, with patrician looks—huge eyes, full lips, high cheekbones. Loretta had been in the movies since she was a child. Her mother, Gladys, ran a boardinghouse for actors when she was younger, and later became a highly regarded decorator who did houses for movie people; she also owned a lot of property. Loretta's three sisters were all quite beautiful—one, Georgiana, married Ricardo Montalban and had a lengthy and successful marriage, while another one, Sally Blane, also had a decent acting career. Douglas Fairbanks Jr. went out with Sally for a while, and made a batch of movies with Loretta at Warners; like everybody else she was close to, he called her "Gretch," short for her real name.

Loretta used to claim that her mother didn't care all that much about the movie industry. Gladys once told her daughter, "I don't understand how you can be an actress—the people are so rude. The men don't even know enough to stand up from their desks when you walk into a room."

Of course, this posture of noblesse oblige raises the question of why all four of Gladys's daughters went into the movies if their mother was so indifferent toward the industry. Part of it was that Loretta's father disappeared when she was about four years old; the family had to have some money coming in, and acting was as good a way as any other, and more lucrative than most. I think the only time all the girls worked together was in *The Story of Alexander Graham Bell*, with Don Ameche and Henry Fonda. Since there was such a strong family resemblance, they could only play sisters, which rather limited the opportunities for the other girls.

But none of them got close to the career Loretta had because none of them cared as much or worked as hard. Once, when one of her sisters showed up in a movie wearing a bad hairstyle, Loretta read her the riot act. Her sister protested that her hairstylist had insisted it would look good, and Loretta snapped, "If you don't know more than your hair-stylist, you don't deserve to have one."

Loretta herself started playing juvenile leads shortly after reaching puberty, and by 1928, when she was only about fifteen, she was working with Lon Chaney at MGM.

She once told me that Chaney had been patient with her when she was a very nervous girl. Once he asked her, "Gretchen, do you like milkshakes?"

She said yes, and then he asked her what kind.

"Vanilla."

So he suggested that whenever she looked at him during a scene, she should think of vanilla milkshakes. Lon Chaney was obviously a good guy who could cope with a young actress's inexperience by talking to her as if she were a child, which Loretta basically was. Unfortunately, Herbert Brenon, the director, wasn't as indulgent. He once threw a chair at her.

Stanwyck and Crawford came up the hard way, which couldn't really be said of Loretta. But the life of a young actress in Hollywood is never easy, and people devise various methods of coping. Loretta's armor was her Catholicism and her reputation for being a *grande dame*.

She certainly lived up to her billing. I had heard about her swear box on her sets, but I didn't really believe it until I saw it with my own eyes. Anybody who cut loose with a burst of profanity, whether it was a grip or a costar, was obligated to drop some money into the box. At the end of the week, Loretta donated the proceeds to a Catholic charity.

The end result of all this was that people watched their language and everything else around her. She was regarded as one of the true ladies of the movies, although her offscreen life indicated she was perfectly capable of dropping her rosary when the occasion demanded.

I've written before about the way the studios controlled the information that reached the public. When they wanted to, they could enforce a lockdown the Central Intelligence Agency would envy. But within the

Loretta Young

industry, secrets were impossible to keep. People heard stories, people gossiped. Often, the information came directly from the parties involved.

Everybody knew who was gay, and with very few exceptions, everybody knew who was having an affair, and with whom. An actress who was stepping out with her leading man would mention something to her hairdresser, who would mention it to his boyfriend, who would promptly call Hedda or Louella, who would run a blind item that nobody outside the business could decipher but that served as a sharp jab in the ribs to everyone in the business.

For years my publicist was a woman named Helen Ferguson, who had been an actress in the silent days and then segued into publicity when the parts got scarce. Helen was also the publicist and close friend of Barbara Stanwyck's, who suggested I hire her—one of my smarter moves. Besides impeccably managing things for me, Helen would often treat me to some of the inside dope she was privy to.

So, one way or the other, we all heard the story about Loretta's illegitimate child from her brief affair with Clark Gable. They had met on the location of the aptly named *Call of the Wild* in 1935, which was made at Fox by William Wellman.

It was not Loretta's first fling with a married man. There had been an affair with Spencer Tracy a few years earlier, but pregnancy involved an entirely different level of complication. Because she was a strict Catholic, Loretta wouldn't get an abortion. In those days, actresses who became pregnant went to the hospital for what would be announced as "an appendectomy" or "exhaustion." Some must have had serious stamina issues, because they were hospitalized for exhaustion every couple of years.

For her part, Loretta went away on a lengthy vacation, had the child, stashed her in an orphanage, and then doubled back and adopted her, naming her Judy. It was a neat end around, and it wasn't the first time that gambit was pulled. Years earlier, William de Mille, the brother of Cecil B. and a good director in his own right, as well as a very married man, got his girlfriend pregnant. She went away and had the baby, a boy, whereupon Cecil adopted the child. He simply couldn't stomach the idea of a DeMille being cast out into the world, illegitimate or not. Besides, Cecil's children were girls, and he liked the idea of having a boy around the house. William's wife didn't know the truth, nor did his daughter Agnes, who later became a famous choreographer, nor did Cecil's own children.

Cecil and William struck a bargain that the boy—Cecil named him Richard—would only be told the true story of his parentage when one of the brothers died. Richard went through the first thirty-odd years of his life thinking he was an anonymous foundling who got lucky. It wasn't until William de Mille died in 1955 that he learned the truth, rocking him to his core.

The true story of Judy Lewis's birth never leaked out until years later, after Clark had died, and Judy wrote a book about her exceedingly strange upbringing. How did she find out the truth? Her fiancé told her two weeks before they got married. The publication of the book resulted in Loretta's not speaking to her daughter for more than ten years.

Even before that, though, the real account was widely accepted in Hollywood, mostly because anyone who met Judy couldn't help but be struck by her strong resemblance to her father—she had his broad face, his warm eyes, and early in her life, his jug ears. The ears were a real problem, so Loretta had Judy undergo plastic surgery on them when she was only seven years old.

I spent some time with Judy when she was an adult, and she was a lovely person. She couldn't have had an easy childhood. For Loretta, Judy was a reminder of her having strayed from the straight and narrow path, so she was less than affectionate with the child. "Remember, you're a reflection of me," she would tell her. Although Judy carried the surname of Lewis—Loretta's husband, whom she married years after she had Judy, was named Tom Lewis—her stepfather never actually adopted her.

Judy met her real father precisely once, when she was about fifteen, and her mother and Clark were making another movie together, called *Key to the City*. Judy came home one day to find Clark sitting in the living room of her home. They had the usual chitchat—he asked her about school, boys she was seeing—and after a while, he said he had to go. She walked him to the door, he kissed her on the forehead, and he left. She never saw him again.

The interesting thing was that whenever the subject of Clark would come up, Loretta didn't have all that much good to say about him. "Clark Gable . . . to me, was not so much an actor as he was a star," she once remarked, years after Clark's death. "Spencer Tracy . . . was such a magnificent actor that he was also a star, but he was never the star that Clark Gable was, because he didn't have, I guess, the magnitude or the sex appeal or whatever you want to call it that Clark Gable had."

I believe that is referred to as passive aggression.

Judy worked on Loretta's TV show for a few years, then became an actress herself. In her forties, she went back to college and became a clinical psychologist with a specialty in marriage and family therapy, helping to untie the emotional knots that her own family had never been able to articulate, let alone deal with.

Recently Loretta's daughter-in-law gave an interview in which she announced that Loretta had told her that Judy Lewis was the result of rape; that a drunk Clark Gable had come into Loretta's train compartment on the way back to Hollywood and forced himself on her.

Well.

In response to that retroactive piece of character assassination, I can say that I knew Bill Wellman quite well, and he was firmly convinced that Clark and Loretta were having an affair during the making of the film, to the extent that it became a detriment to the movie.

Besides that, I knew Clark Gable, and he simply wasn't the kind of man to force himself on a woman. At least one woman who knew whereof she spoke told me that he was very courtly, a complete gentleman of a type that was rarely found in Hollywood, or, for that matter, anywhere else. Clark and Loretta didn't have any choice about how

they dealt with the matter of their out-of-wedlock child. Today, unmarried people can have children and nobody thinks anything of it, but
in the 1930s, 1940s, and 1950s, an illegitimate birth would have destroyed a star's career, as Ingrid Bergman discovered when she became
pregnant by Roberto Rossellini. She was denounced in Congress—as
if it were anybody's business but Ingrid's—and was ostracized by
Hollywood for years until things cooled down.

Loretta had to be petrified during her entire pregnancy; not only
her career, but the well-being of her entire family, whom she supported
to a great degree, hung in the balance. Given what she had gone
through, and that she had made the same decision as Ingrid—to pro-
ceed with the pregnancy—Loretta might have considered standing up
for Bergman, but she kept silent.

Neither her pregnancy nor anything else ever seemed to faze Loretta.

She had epic battles with Darryl Zanuck when she was under contract at Fox. Darryl used to grouse that she continually rejected the
costumes he chose for her by saying, "I'm a fashion plate. I don't care
whether you like it or not. I am known as one of the best-dressed
women in motion pictures."

"My wife wouldn't wear a dress like that," Darryl retorted, which
she followed with a withering, impolitic put-down: "Your wife isn't a
movie star. *I* am." As the argument escalated, she torched the bridge:
"You ruin every woman you touch." It wasn't long before Loretta left
Fox, to the great relief of both her and Zanuck.

Loretta was one tough lady. Her sister Sally said, "She didn't seem
to mind rejection like I did. She didn't take it personally. . . . Any rejection she got just made Loretta more determined. 'What do they know?'
she would say."

Loretta was well positioned in the business socially as well as psychologically, and she managed her career with great canniness. She was
a movie star for thirty-five years, and when movie roles began to dry
up in the early 1950s, she simply segued to television.

She explained what made her switch mediums: She and the family were watching TV, a suspense program. A woman walked into a dark room and started to get undressed. The camera moved in on her until she was in close-up, whereupon two hands came into the shot and strangled her. Loretta's children started to cry, because they'd never seen a murder in their living room before.

With that, Loretta decided to do a show that wouldn't scare viewers, but would inspire and elevate them instead, and had great success for nearly ten years. As always, she was smart about how she approached the matter. At that time, a network program involved making more than thirty episodes a year. Loretta realized that they all couldn't be good, and set her criteria at ten good shows annually.

The Loretta Young Show, which began airing in 1953, rehearsed for two days and was shot in three. Loretta found that she liked the pace, that doing that much production, that much work, sped up her metabolism and was perfectly capable of making her a better actress than she had been.

At the time she went into television, it was regarded as a huge step down from the movies, so a lot of tongue clucking went on. Dore Schary, who was running MGM at the time, told her she was making a big mistake and would never get a job in the movies again.

But Loretta went ahead anyway. Her reasoning was simple: "I couldn't pick my own roles in the movies. When I had my TV show, that's when I had a good time." I think that finally attaining absolute control was a factor in her happiness. She also felt that after winning an Oscar for *The Farmer's Daughter*, there was nowhere to go but down in the movie business.

On her show, an anthology series, Loretta played everything from nuns to hookers to Chinese wives. Each story had a moral, which she reemphasized in her farewell at its end. Another trademark of the show was her entrance at the beginning of every episode, in which she sashayed through a doorway in a gorgeous gown. It was very glamorous, but it made Loretta ripe for parody. Imogene Coca did a hilarious bit playing her, trying to waft through the doorway, only to get her dress wedged. Watching Coca try to get her dress unstuck while maintaining her gracious smile and serene composure was priceless.

How smart was Loretta? She got to keep all the dresses.

The emphasis on clothes and moral uplift implied that the audience for the show was predominantly female, and her audience was extremely loyal. The show ran into the early 1960s, although it doesn't get revived today—the only black-and-white half-hour TV shows that really survive are *The Honeymooners*, *I Love Lucy*, and *The Twilight Zone*. For modern audiences, Loretta's career basically ends in 1953, even though she continued to make very occasional TV appearance into the 1980s.

It was a very long run for an actress who was more highly regarded for her luminous beauty than as an acting talent, her Oscar notwithstanding. But she maintained her looks as assiduously as she maintained her career, and a fifty-year stand at or near the top of show business is not to be underestimated.

The amazing thing about Loretta is that she walked away with nary a tremor. She had done it all and decided to get out while the getting was good. I think her religion insulated her from the normal insecurity that afflicts people in the acting profession.

After you retire, there is really only one question: How do you fill the days? But Loretta had always regulated her life—movies were a component, and in time movies were replaced by TV, and after that she turned to religious activism and to being the perfect hostess. She always insisted that she had lived her personal life concurrently with her professional life, and that's certainly possible—Loretta and Irene Dunne were cut from the same bolt of cloth, except I think Irene actually practiced her religion to a deeper extent.

If Loretta had a weakness, it was her conventional taste in scripts as well as performance. Opposite Orson Welles in his film *The Stranger*, she plays a woman who unknowingly marries an escaped Nazi war criminal. After she stumbles upon the truth, she has one great line: "When you kill me, don't touch me!"

The line needs to be read with defiance, with theatrical

bravura—imagine what Stanwyck or Davis would have done with it—
but Loretta didn't have the temperament for the big moment. She had
great strength in her own life, but not when it came to the work—she
always wanted to be, *had* to be, a lady. She plays the moment down, and
the scene doesn't have the kick it should have.

There might have been a gap between what Loretta actually was
and how she wished to be perceived, but that's not unusual in the general population, let alone the movie business.

How she managed to reconcile her piety with the fact of her illegitimate daughter is a question nobody has ever answered. But she kept her
chin high and sailed through life with the appearance of complete
self-assurance.

THE FORTIES

While many of the actresses of the 1930s were virtual goddesses, World War II started a vogue for more approachable women, who might be categorized as girls next door.

These could range from June Allyson to Betty Hutton, Teresa Wright to Donna Reed. I've always suspected that MGM's Andy Hardy films played a big role in developing this public taste. Even though they were modestly budgeted B movies, the Hardy films were hugely popular, and the studio had a policy of dropping newly signed ingénues into them. The acting bar was set low enough that none of them would be embarrassed by her performance; all any of them had to do was be charming and hold the camera.

The other studios saw how young actresses like Judy Garland, Donna Reed, and Lana Turner were embraced by audiences and began developing their own rosters of wholesome starlets. Personally, if I ever saw Donna Reed walking her dog anywhere near my house, I would have immediately moved next door.

To an extent, I've been writing about success stories, but the truth of the movie business is that it often attracts people who have innate instabilities, and the experience of the industry only widens the fault lines in their personalities. I'd be less than honest if I didn't discuss some of the sadder lives that I came across.

Betty Hutton always acted as if she'd been shot out of a cannon— she was the female version of wild men like Mickey Rooney or Harry Ritz or, if you prefer, a WASP version of Carmen Miranda. This was fine when there was a war on and there was a great deal of anxiety to be displaced. But after the war, she seemed out of tempo with the times and her career ended quickly. From a rapid rise to an even more rapid fall, Hutton's career ran for just about ten years.

But she will remain important in film history if only because in 1944 she made *The Miracle of Morgan's Creek* for Preston Sturges, a film that inspires one single question: How did they get away with it?

Hutton plays Trudy Kockenlocker, a small-town girl who *really* likes soldiers. So much so that she goes on a date, gets drunk, and gets pregnant by a GI whose name she can only remember as something like "Ratzkywatzky." (Sturges does throw in a quick line about a hurry-up wedding, but if you blink you'll miss it.)

Trudy needs a husband, and fast, so her mortified father enlists Eddie Bracken, who was the 1940s version of Harold Lloyd—shy, sweet, meaning well at all times, and a bit nervous.

It's an amazing film—amazingly accomplished, amazingly audacious—and Hutton is remarkable in it. Trudy is far from self-aware, but she's sincere. In spite of the fact that the movie is a raucous farce, you're pulling for her if for no other reason than she'd be a great mother. Scattered, but great.

Nobody realized it at the time, but Betty Hutton was doing something extraordinary: embodying female energy unleashed. After the Sturges film, she starred in some successful musicals, stepped in when Judy Garland couldn't make it through *Annie Get Your Gun* at MGM, and was one of the stars of DeMille's *The Greatest Show on Earth*.

It was right around the time of the DeMille film that I went over to Paramount to see some friends. When the conversation turned to Betty, I was shown a large sandbag up in the flies of the soundstage that had her name painted on it, with an arrow pointing downward. The stagehands had amused themselves by fantasizing an arcane way of killing Hutton. My friends proceeded to tell me how heartily Hutton was disliked by the studio rank and file, not to mention the front office.

It seemed that she was a prima donna, nasty to underlings, and generally a deeply unpleasant person. I was a young actor at the time, and

Betty Hutton

I went away determined to be the kind of actor who the crew liked and respected. Besides that, I was not eager to have a sandbag drop anywhere in my vicinity.

It would take thirty years for the rest of the world, and for women in general, to even begin to catch up to what Betty Hutton was representing in *The Miracle of Morgan's Creek*, and by that time she was out of show business and living as a housekeeper in the rectory of a Catholic church in Rhode Island.

It was the culmination of a long slide down that neither she nor anybody else seemed able to stop. She walked out of her Paramount contract when they wouldn't let her choreographer husband direct one of her pictures, and if that sandbag was any indication, the studio was glad to see her go. A number of TV specials failed, so did a series, and so did her marriages—all four of them—until finally, there was a complete breakdown.

Hutton made only one more public appearance, with my friend Robert Osborne on Turner Classic Movies. She was so fragile, so tremulous— she looked as though she might collapse at any moment. When she died in Palm Springs in 2007, she was living on Social Security in a very modest apartment and estranged from her three children.

There wasn't enough money to bury Betty Hutton, so the undertaker called Watson Webb, another friend of mine who had been a premiere film editor at 20th Century Fox. Watson was one of the few editors to have a gold membership card in his union, and was independently wealthy.

The undertaker knew Watson had been in the movie business and thought he might have some idea whom to call. Watson didn't bother calling anybody; he wrote a check to cover the cost of Betty's burial. He had never even met her, but he did it because somebody had to take care of a poor woman who had once been a great star. That's the sort of man he was.

If you wrote the story of Betty Hutton's life as a novel, nobody would believe it, and it would be so depressing that nobody would want to read it. But for one magical movie, she and Preston Sturges united to make a stunningly original comedy that said something serious about the country and where it would be headed.

I can't say that I knew Gene Tierney particularly well—I never worked with her, although she was at Fox at the same time I was, and we would chat then and afterward.

Gene was very slender and slightly built; she looked as if a stiff wind could pick her up and deposit her in the next county. But I remember how beautifully she moved—like a dancer, as if invisible wires running through her shoulders carried the weight of her body. She was angelically beautiful.

On-screen, Gene had a serenity that rarely cracked. Even when she played a psychopath in *Leave Her to Heaven*, she conveyed the complete assurance of someone who was used to having her plans work out. Which was pretty much Gene in her personal life as well. She was born into money and was educated at private schools in Connecticut and Europe. When she told her father that she was interested in becoming an actress, he formed a family-owned corporation to promote her.

She appeared in a couple of Broadway plays and was signed for the movies by Darryl Zanuck by the time she was twenty-one. Gene photographed like a sleek Siamese cat, but didn't give that impression in person, where her fragility was more apparent. As a person, I found her deliberate to the point of lethargy.

Gene's great tragedy occurred during World War II. She was on a bond-selling tour when she contracted German measles from a woman who got out of a sickbed to meet her favorite actress. Unfortunately, Gene was pregnant at the time, and her child was born severely retarded. Gene's husband, Oleg Cassini, did all the right things, supporting his wife and paying for the child's care, but the marriage broke up.

The birth of Gene's daughter precipitated a series of mental collapses; she had had at least one breakdown before I arrived at the studio.

Gene Tierney

At one point, she was institutionalized for a year and a half. Scuttlebutt around the studio said that she was at the Menninger Clinic, and the general attitude around Fox was that she was damaged. It was my first experience with an unofficial attitude of surveillance—it was as if the entire studio were watching Gene out of the corner of its collective eye to see if she was going to shatter into a million pieces.

At that time, mental illness was not discussed, and stars were kept at a safe remove from media scrutiny. Now, of course, we know that a stint in rehab or even a breakdown can be finessed into a story of personal triumph, a way to reboot a career. But in those days, it was thought that the truth about various issues that were every bit as frequent then as they are now would cause the public's affection for a given star to disappear overnight.

Darryl Zanuck was caught in a bind. On the one hand, he was an emotional man who would always be supportive when one of his employees was having a problem. On the other, he had to move thirty pictures a year off the Fox stages and into theaters, so his sympathy had something of a clock on it. If you were going to work with troubled people—an apt description of a lot of the inhabitants of show business—you had to walk a fine line.

Gene segued out of the movie business in the mid-1950s, married an oilman, and, except for a few guest appearances, lived the rest of her life in Texas. Everybody who knew her hoped she achieved some measure of peace.

Linda Darnell was another woman who had a sad end. I knew Linda quite well. Obviously, she was strikingly beautiful, but as I got to know her I also discovered her kindness and consideration for other people. My impression of Linda was that she was deeply ambivalent about a career in the movies. The child of a stage mother, she had been entered in beauty contests since she was twelve. Linda looked older than she was, and was playing ingénue roles in the movies by the time she was sixteen or so.

There was a placidity about Linda, but Darryl Zanuck figured out a way to make it work on-screen. She ultimately became a big star because Darryl cast her in huge films that were almost guaranteed to be hits, like *Forever Amber*. But she also fronted ordinary programmers and sold them with her sincerity and beauty, as well as the occasional project that was actually of high quality, like *A Letter to Three Wives* and *My Darling Clementine*.

But by the end of the 1940s, Linda had begun to put on some weight, and she either couldn't or wouldn't take it off—the added pounds might have been her passive-aggressive tactic for getting out of a business she never wanted to be in. Darryl dropped her, and her career began a rapid descent. Just as she had seemed to be in her twenties when she was still a teenager, now she seemed to be in her forties while still in her early thirties.

Linda went on to work in occasional TV shows and dinner theater until she died in a house fire in 1965. She deserved better from the movies, and from life.

Just as Betty Grable had been hired by Zanuck as a possible replacement for Alice Faye, so June Haver was hired as a possible replacement for Betty Grable. I got to know June even before I got to Fox, and the story of our meeting gives some indication of her quality as a human being.

When I arrived at Fox, bumptious kid that I was, I asked her if she would come to a party at my high school. She said yes! I danced with her, and nobody took their eyes off us for the entire night. She was a great, classy lady, a terrific person. She was also talented, but her films never had the commercial impact of Grable's. June was a midwestern girl who had been working on stage since she was six years old. By the time she made her first movie in 1943, she was an all-around talent— she could sing, dance, act, you name it.

Her first feature was *The Gang's All Here*, the legendary Busby Berkeley movie with Carmen Miranda, the giant bananas, and Alice Faye moaning "No Love, No Nothin'." Darryl slotted June into a

Linda Darnell

succession of musicals and rural comedies, most of which were quite popular.

But June was unhappy. In 1953, she announced she was retiring from films to become a nun. A short while later, she left the convent and married Fred MacMurray, whose first wife had committed suicide. June and Fred adopted a couple of kids and spent the rest of their lives together. Today their daughter Kate runs an excellent winery that she built on land Fred owned.

Fred and June were extremely happy together. Fred was a great guy with one personality quirk—he was one of the tightest people with a buck I've ever met. Watching him leave twenty-five-cent tips constituted one of Hollywood's most harrowing experiences. Not surprisingly, he became extremely wealthy, but the comfort his money provided was paltry compared to the satisfaction he took in his good marriage. Years after June went with me to the school dance, we worked up a soft-shoe routine for a benefit for St. John's Hospital. She could still dance.

During the 1930s and 1940s each studio had a specific physical look to its films. You watch thirty seconds of a movie and know immediately whether it was made by MGM (creamy white light, few shadows) or Paramount (heavy diffusion, more grays than blacks or whites), or Warner Bros. (hardly any whites, mostly grays, fairly realistic).

Similarly, the studios employed different types of actresses, a choice that was usually a function of executive preference combined with audience taste. Louis B. Mayer liked his actresses to represent a certain class and dignity, as exemplified by Garbo, Shearer, Loy, MacDonald, and Garson. There were a few exceptions—most notably Jean Harlow and Marie Dressler, token representatives of the working class. In the 1940s, Lana Turner embodied some of Harlow's working-class sensuality.

It's safe to say that Bette Davis wouldn't have lasted three weeks at

MGM; her career would have been up for grabs the first time she sailed into Mayer's office in a state of high dudgeon and upbraided him for his terrible taste in scripts.

Greer Garson, in contrast, was deferential to the studio, and MGM responded by casting her in a string of lavish showcases that proved to be huge hits: *Mrs. Miniver, Pride and Prejudice, Random Harvest, Madame Curie,* and *Mrs. Parkington.* Eight of her films paired her with Walter Pidgeon, and they were the most reassuring of screen teams, if a trifle elderly. During World War II, audiences were comforted by their solidity. These films made amazing amounts of money, and Garson was one of the key box office stars of the war years.

Her days of huge hits ended soon afterward, however—the social changes wrought by World War II made her screen character seem insufferably noble, and she was unable or unwilling to add much earthiness to the mixture. By 1947 or so, she began to seem starchy.

But Mayer had given Garson a cast-iron contract, so she kept making expensive but money-losing pictures for MGM well into the 1950s. Greer Garson isn't spoken of much today, but if you want to understand America just before and during World War II, you need to understand her and the appeal of her genteel goodness.

I met Greer when I was just a boy working at the Bel-Air Stables. She lived right across the street from the stables, and she and Richard Ney, her husband at the time, came over frequently to ride. Because it was wartime, all the grooms were working at airplane factories, so twelve- and thirteen-year-old kids got jobs that would ordinarily have gone to adults. After riding, Greer and Richard would both have tea.

Their marriage raised eyebrows—Ney had played Greer's son in *Mrs. Miniver* and was about ten years younger than she was. Richard was a smart and interesting man, but an indistinct actor; with the exception of a couple of for-old-times'-sake appearances for friends, he left the movie business around 1950 to become a successful Wall Street investor.

Years later, I got to know Greer all over again, by which time she

Greer Garson

was married to a Texas oilman named Buddy Fogelson and was living in Palm Springs near the Eldorado Country Club, which Buddy helped found. After playing Eleanor Roosevelt in *Sunrise at Campobello*, Greer dialed back to enjoy life with Buddy and to attend to various philanthropies in and around Texas, which became her adopted home.

I loved Greer and always thought it curious that the roles she typically played were so far removed from who she actually was as a person. She was at all times very English, with a passion for French poodles and a quite lively, sometimes bawdy sense of humor. Laurence Olivier had discovered her and told me he thought she was very talented. Errol Flynn worked with her in a good MGM movie called *That Forsyte Woman* and remembered her in surprising terms: "Greer Garson was the first actress I worked with who was fun." (Take *that*, Olivia and Bette!)

Offscreen, Greer enjoyed a good time. Like the vast majority of the women I got to know in the movie business, she had innate drive—Hollywood is no place for shrinking violets. When she decided on a course of action, she totally committed to it and found a way to accomplish her goals.

Besides Greer Garson and Walter Pidgeon, MGM's other great screen team of this period was Spencer Tracy and Kate Hepburn. They made nine movies together, six of which cast them as a married couple, five of which characterized those marriages as troubled. This was smart filmmaking, because it echoed their very real differences as people—Kate was a bossy New England Yankee, Spence was a phlegmatic midwesterner.

I first met Kate through Spencer Tracy, with whom I became quite close after we made two pictures together (*Broken Lance* and *The Mountain*). She was great company, of course, and we became good friends. I asked her to be godmother to my eldest daughter, whom I named Kate in her honor.

Like many actors, Kate enjoyed talking about her flops at least as much as she did the great successes. The key ingredient is having overcome the flops; actors who have been damaged by a catastrophic movie or play don't enjoy talking about it any more than old soldiers enjoy talking about losing a leg.

When Kate was in a reminiscent mood, a failure like *Sylvia Scarlett* would get as much time as *The Philadelphia Story*. As with most huge flops, the former film came to have something of a cult following in later years, which didn't cut much mustard with Kate. Her attitude was "Where were they when I needed them?" She told me that Pandro Berman, who was running RKO at the time, was so distraught over the resounding flop of *Sylvia Scarlett* that he told her he never wanted to make another movie with her as long as he lived. He did later, when they were both at MGM, but an actor doesn't forget moments like that.

Kate was somewhat insulated from the vagaries of show business by the fact that her family was well off. She didn't need the movie business the way most of the other actresses I'm talking about did: as a means of financial security. But she was an actress through and through—she loved being adored, she expected to be adored, and she was adored.

The self-possession that radiates from Hepburn on-screen was an authentic part of her personality. She didn't hesitate, she didn't prevaricate, she didn't doubt. She generally got what she wanted, at least partially because of her radiant self-confidence. I always found Kate interesting in that she never thought of herself as being beautiful, not at all; she was quite modest about her looks, and it was a genuine modesty, not a calculated affectation intended to provoke reassurance.

What she knew she did have, and what she had absolute self-confidence in, was her personality. She was well aware that there was nobody else remotely like her, at least not in Hollywood, and that her singularity would carry her through even if her talent failed her. You might not like her as an actress, but you could not disregard her as a woman. She counted on that.

On-screen, Spence and Kate reversed the common explanation about the success of the union of Astaire and Rogers: Spence's earthiness gave Kate sex, and she gave him class. That they were an offscreen couple from their first movie together in 1942 was irrelevant; Spence

Katharine Hepburn

was a married man, and the relationship with Kate was occasionally tense.

The two spent a fair amount of time apart, although I don't believe either of them ever thought of leaving the relationship. On the cellular level, both understood that, despite all the temporary chafings, life for them was unthinkable without the other. The relationship between Kate and Spence was like the relationship between John Wayne and John Ford. With the world at large, Duke Wayne set the agenda; with Ford, he listened to what Ford wanted, then said, "Yes, sir."

Kate was used to getting her way, either through demands or subtler persuasion. But if Spence thought she was talking absolute balls, he'd snap, "Shut up, Kate," and she'd shut up. I was always amazed by her deference, because I knew damn well that as far as Kate Hepburn was concerned, *deference* was just a word in a dictionary, and not one whose meaning she had much interest in learning. Spence was her romantic ideal, but he also had the aura of a father figure to her, someone for whom she had immense respect.

I think the basis of that respect was his unassuming ability as a professional. She thought, as so many of us did, that he was one of the very few great actors in the movie business. She would grumble that George Cukor always gave her notes on her performances, but he hardly ever gave Spence any serious direction. He didn't need to; when Cukor looked at the rushes, everything he wanted to see in Tracy's performance was already there.

It wasn't just that you never caught Spence acting; it's that his acting doesn't date. Acting has styles, just as fashion does; what seems revelatory at the time can seem awfully mannered only a few decades later. But a Tracy performance is as consonant with 2016 as it was with 1945, and there are very few actors of whom that can be said. Only one, actually.

Theirs was an utterly adorable relationship, because the dynamic was completely that of an old married couple, even though they never married. They had that easy back-and-forth rhythm that old married couples have, as well as a sense of genuinely liking each other. The sexual attraction had been joined by a deep friendship, which is the best kind of romantic combination because it will sustain a relationship even if the sex burns out.

They worked well together because they balanced each other. Spence could be solitary and grumpy, and prefer to be left alone. Kate was always a woman who said yes to the next thing, especially if it was something she had never done before. Yes to a movie if it seemed interesting; yes to a Broadway musical, if for no other reason than she had never done a Broadway musical; yes to speaking for the left-wing presidential candidate Henry Wallace in 1948.

Yes to all that life has to offer.

This was the most valuable thing Kate gave me: She was always outward bound—an object lesson in how to live your life.

I worked with Joan Blondell on both *It Takes a Thief* and *Switch*, and her demeanor was very much that of a working actress, a total pro, without any airs. But to me she was show-business royalty—I was thrilled to meet her, let alone act with her.

She came to the movies in 1930, just about eighteen months after it became clear that sound wasn't a fad after all. She had been in a Broadway play with Jimmy Cagney called *Penny Arcade*, and she and Cagney did a screen test for Warner Bros. and headed west immediately thereafter.

Jimmy Cagney told me later about his and Joan's screen test—they knew the scene, because it was from *Penny Arcade*, and they knew each other well because they'd worked together for months at that point. The test crackled with energy and authenticity. Al Jolson had bought the movie rights to the play, and he turned around and sold it to Warners, where he was regarded as practically family because of *The Jazz Singer* and what came after. Of course, when Jolson's box office began to fall off in the early 1930s, he became just another employee, albeit a rich one. With Jack Warner, relationships had a way of being temporary.

Anyway, Jim and Joan were off to Warner Bros. almost immediately on a one-picture contract. Their first movie turned out to be an adaptation of *Penny Arcade* under what Jack Warner believed to be the more commercial title of *Sinners' Holiday*. Joan told me that Jack Warner signed her and Cagney to long-term contracts the day after they started shooting the picture—the rushes were that good.

Joan had been born in a trunk—literally. Her parents were vaudeville troupers, and she told me she spent most of her childhood working in the family act while traveling around America, Europe, China, and Australia. The Blondells played both the Pantages and Orpheum circuits, so you would have to rank them as successful, although Joan never claimed that they played the Palace—the vaudeville equivalent of a command performance before the Royal Family. Suffice it to say that there was no aspect of the business she wouldn't eventually experience and, more important, understand.

Joan had some formal education, but not much; it was snatched a week or a month at a time when the family was on tour, or during brief downtimes. Like a lot of the women in this book, that nominal schooling didn't stop her from being very well read. Toward the end of her life, she even wrote a novel called *Center Door Fancy*, which was more or less about her childhood in vaudeville, and it's something she should justifiably have been proud of—it's a good book. Joan was savvy, with huge street smarts.

The question arises as to whether the lack of formal education was a deterrent for some of these women, not so much in their careers—they could hire accountants to handle their money, and agents to help make career decisions—but in life. I feel qualified to offer an opinion about this because I only graduated from high school myself, after which I immediately began my assault on the fortress of show business.

Honestly, I don't think it matters. In show business you are exposed

Joan Blondell

to people, places, and situations that you could never dream of encoun-
tering in college, and in fact never would encounter in a conventional
career. Some of those people and places and situations are good, and
some are far from good, but show business has always seemed to me to
be the equivalent not just of college, but of an exhaustively demanding
graduate school.

Speaking for myself, I believe that I got far more out of 20th Century Fox than I ever would have gotten out of USC. What really matters is the desire to learn. If that's present, and you have some personal
initiative, you'll do just fine in show business and, I suspect, in life.

Joan was one of those actresses whose essential nature came through
the lens. She quickly became very popular in movies like *Public Enemy*
(Cagney again), *Gold Diggers of 1933*, and *Footlight Parade* (Cagney
again). She typically played a streetwise sweetheart of a girl, almost
always working class, a waitress or a chorus girl who was maybe a little
brassy, but with a big heart. Audiences liked her, and Jack Warner liked
her, too—Joan worked in as many as ten pictures a year.

Being employed by Warners was like finding yourself in the middle
of a large, contentious family operation whose members had a tendency
toward loud squabbling. I remember her once telling me that because
they routinely worked very long days—to get a picture finished on
schedule could mean an eighteen- or twenty-hour shift on the last day
or two of a shoot—the relationships on set became like being with your
parents and uncles and aunts. The flow of work was so long and the
Warners stock company so unchanging that sometimes they wouldn't
even say hello or good-bye in the morning or at night. The crews became family, and some of the actors did, too.

If you asked her about those great Warners musicals, she'd respond
by talking about how much effort they involved—much more than the
straight comedies or dramas. There were no unions in the early 1930s,
which meant that you'd have to be at the studio by six in the morning to
go into makeup, and you might not break for lunch until three in the

afternoon, which meant that you wouldn't get out of there until midnight or close to it.

"You'd be ready to collapse," Joan recalled.

On Saturday, you'd work all night, sometimes till the sun came up on Sunday. Even though everybody was young, it was still exhausting. And of course, such rampant abuse just hastened the arrival of unions in a couple of years.

"Time off?" she told me. "We didn't have time off. Jack got his money's worth. If you weren't acting, you were rehearsing a number, or you were doing a photo layout. When I got pregnant, they kept me working until I was seven months pregnant. They'd put a chair or a desk in front of me to block out my stomach. That was just the way it was.

"I made quite a few pictures that I never even saw because I was too busy working. And decades later I'd see one on TV and I honestly wouldn't remember making it, even though the evidence was right there in front of me."

I have no doubt Joan was telling the truth. She would laugh when I asked her about the nightlife, because how could you possibly work those hours and go out at night? By the time Busby Berkeley was through shooting a musical number, the nightclubs were about to close!

The primary difference between Joan as a performer and Joan as a woman was that she was actually very domestic, and preferred being at home to being out in public. She was devoted to acting, but when she wasn't performing, the last thing she wanted to do was go out on the town or pose for publicity photos. She would explain that when she was in vaudeville, the itinerant nature of her family's profession meant that there was no such thing as a home life. The reason she played shopgirls or waitresses so well is that the vaudeville life was the show-business equivalent: You made a living, but it was a precarious one. Because Joan had traveled incessantly for the first twenty years or so of her life, as an adult she valued the nest as much as any woman I've ever known.

Her big dramatic break was probably Elia Kazan's *A Tree Grows in*

Brooklyn, which came after she left Warners, in which she gives a beautiful performance as Aunt Sissy. (It's a very good movie; if you haven't seen it, do yourself a favor.) Joan also did great character work in the classic noir *Nightmare Alley*, opposite Tyrone Power. In my experience, Aunt Sissy was Joan to a T, except Joan was more maternal than brassy; in the vernacular of the 1930s, she was a great broad.

I had seen many of Joan's movies, loved them and her, and she didn't disappoint me when we worked together. On the set, she was a very accomplished actress, with a terrific, humorous style that was all her own. She was fun and vivacious, and would often share little flashes, moments that stood out from the blur of making so many movies and making them so quickly. She once told me about working in *Public Enemy*, the movie that made Cagney a huge star. Jean Harlow also appeared in the picture in a scene or two, and everyone was very impressed because she was on loan from MGM, and people from MGM barely deigned to speak to people at Warners, let alone work with them.

Anyway, Harlow never wore a bra, and one day she bounced past Cagney, who gave her his wolfish grin and asked, "How do you hold those things up?"

"I ice 'em," she said.

Over the years, Joan was married to some very interesting guys: George Barnes—an excellent cameraman who worked with everybody from Valentino to DeMille. Barnes was followed by Dick Powell, then Mike Todd.

She may have been bruised by the marriages, and I know she was damaged by Todd, who gambled away a lot of her money. She didn't marry again after she and Todd split in 1950, although she was always a very attractive woman. But I don't think there was any bitterness in Joan—it wasn't in her character.

Dick Powell directed a movie I was in called *The Hunters*, so he naturally came up in my conversations with Joan. She said he was a nice guy—very true—but cheap about everything, up to and including lightbulbs and toilet paper. It got to her, and she decided to check out from the marriage in 1945. She spoke of him with humorous exasperation, not anger.

By the time I came to know her, Joan was very easy about her career and where she had arrived professionally. That was unusual, because it can be difficult for an actress who has been a big star to gradually settle for character parts. Sylvia Sidney, who was almost an exact contemporary of Joan's, was well known as an irascible pain in the ass both on and off the set in her later years, which is probably one reason why she didn't work a lot.

But Joan loved the atmosphere of a set, loved actors, loved the process of acting, and considered herself lucky to be in show business, which is probably why she continued working right up to her death.

Long after actresses who had been even bigger stars than she were relegated to menial parts in some pretty grim movies, you could see Joan in quality films like *The Cincinnati Kid,* with her old Warners' pal Edward G. Robinson, or on TV in *Here Come the Brides,* an adaptation of *Seven Brides for Seven Brothers.*

The year before she died she did a movie for John Cassavetes called *Opening Night,* and even though Cassavetes's world was far removed from Joan's, she acquitted herself nobly.

Joan got nominated for an Oscar, as well as several Emmys, but never won. No matter. I honor her in my memory, and she continues to flourish for all those who see her in reruns of her great movies. She was a doll, and a very underrated performer.

Claire Trevor became a star a few years after Joan and a dear friend of mine long before she appeared in *The Mountain* opposite Spencer Tracy and me. She was later welcomed as a member of our inner circle when she played Natalie's mother in *Marjorie Morningstar.*

I had gone to school with the children of Milton Bren, who was Claire's third husband. Milton had custody of his sons from his first marriage, and he and Claire raised them together. Claire became part of my adolescence through her stepsons.

She was another of the actresses who had to go to work as a child. She was a Brooklyn girl, born in Bensonhurst, and attended the American Academy of Dramatic Arts. She began making shorts for Warner Bros. at their studio in the Flatbush section of Brooklyn, and then went to Hollywood.

Claire was warm about almost everything, funny about almost everything. She was particularly merciless about her own pretensions as a young actress, when, she said, she would much rather go to a party than study her part. "I really didn't work very hard," she admitted.

She got parts in some Broadway shows, but it didn't wise her up. She could be hilarious about her lack of foresight. "I got offers from three different studios," she said, "and I turned them all down. The movies were beneath me. Can you imagine being that stupid?"

Then things went cold in New York, and Claire had a very bad period that lasted about six months. No work, no money, no nothing. At that point Fox came back and again offered her a contract, and this time she jumped at it.

The first picture that earned her any notice was *Dead End*, on loan to Sam Goldwyn and William Wyler. She played a hard-up hooker and got an Oscar nomination. You would think that kind of notice would have changed things for her, but she went back to Fox and B pictures, where she was typically cast as a newspaperwoman or a girl detective— playing parts that had previously been given to Glenda Farrell.

But *Dead End* might have been the movie that got her *Stagecoach* for John Ford—again in the role of a prostitute, but one with a sweetness and good heart beneath her tough shell. It was a great performance for a great director, and to the end of her life she would say that it was the best movie she ever made. "The script was excellent," she told me, "the director was the best in the business, the score was good, the camerawork was superb, and the cast couldn't have been improved. Everything jelled, everybody jelled.

Claire Trevor

"It hardly ever happens that way—you always have to make allowances for something in almost every movie. The script isn't quite good enough, or there's an actor who isn't quite right, or something. But *Stagecoach* was one of those rare pictures where everybody was at the top of their game. The pieces all fit."

Claire tried to avoid watching her own movies—she rarely liked her own performance and usually found something lacking in the film itself. But when she watched *Stagecoach*, she fell into the movie just like a member of the audience; she almost forgot she was in it.

She was particularly disappointed with *The High and the Mighty*, because some flashbacks she appeared in were cut—the movie was running long, and something had to go. She felt that losing those scenes meant that her character didn't make much sense, because the audience never saw what had happened to her before she got on the endangered plane that is the center of the film's plot. (All actors have stories about a movie that could have been much better, at least regarding their character or their performance. I think it relates to their basic lack of control in the movie business.)

The same thing happened when she made *Honky Tonk* at MGM, when a couple of her scenes with Clark Gable were cut because the studio wanted to throw the weight of the movie behind Lana Turner. Lana was under contract to MGM, whereas Claire was freelancing, so the studio had no investment in her success. She would talk about how distraught she got over that—she really believed it would damage her career.

She needn't have worried; she would later receive an Academy Award for her turn as the alcoholic mistress of Eddie Robinson's thug in *Key Largo*, and she worked into the 1980s.

What Claire really wanted were those juicy melodramas that Bette Davis did at Warners, but those didn't come her way. She felt she usually had to try to breathe life into parts that basically didn't have much depth. "I'd never met anyone like the women I usually played," she told me. "I had to imagine what they'd be like."

But imagination was one of Claire's strong points as an actress. If the script didn't offer her any help, she'd construct an imaginary biography for the role she was playing—where she was born, how her parents raised her—and then she would project herself into that person with that background and those experiences. That helped her give a sense of someone with a deeper character than the scriptwriter had provided.

Milton Bren's primary business was real estate development, and he became extremely wealthy. He owned *The Pursuit*, a beautiful racing sailboat that won all sorts of races and that he docked at Newport Beach. Milton and Claire and Natalie and I would regularly go to Catalina on Milton's boat. He was a great sailor and became a good producer.

Claire had a sense of inquisitiveness, and of wonder. To her dying day, she was interested in every aspect of life. She always had her painting—she did a portrait of Natalie and me that my daughter Katie now has—her travel, her reading, her friends. Claire was a man's woman. Duke Wayne was crazy about her and valued her highly, and she was also close to Bogart.

Like everyone else, Claire had her ration of grief; Milton died in 1979, just about the same time Duke Wayne did. But the great tragedy came before that: the loss of her son, Charles, who was killed in an airplane crash. It was a terrible blow, but Claire decided that she could sit around and be depressed or get out and enjoy the rest of her life. She bought an apartment at the Pierre in New York and attended every Broadway and museum opening with her close friend Arlene Francis.

I saw Claire for the last time just before she died, and she was still clearheaded, still a woman of absolute honesty and warmth—a straight-up woman, the very best kind.

When she died, Claire left $5,000 each to several dozen friends. I was one of them; her will said to "consider this a hug and a kiss." Whenever I'm in Paris, I still go to the caviar bar she took me to. Then I drink a toast to Claire's memory and do it all over again. It's been on my tab for a long time, but I will always be in debt to this extraordinary actress, this woman who helped teach me how to live an affirmative life.

Looking back, I can see that Claire became a valued mentor for me because of my admiration for her talent as an actress and her warmth as a human being. She was an Earth Mother: bountiful, loving, always supportive. Show business gave her the leverage and the wherewithal to educate herself, and she and Barbara Stanwyck both stressed the importance of using it as a vehicle to build a life outside of the movie business.

I miss her every day.

Jack Warner wouldn't have had a clue about how to showcase Greer Garson or Greta Garbo. Because he was a rough-and-tumble mug himself, he filled his studio with people of a similar persuasion—Cagney, Davis, Flynn, George Raft, Eddie Robinson, people who loved to treat Jack with the complete lack of respect he craved.

Over at 20th Century Fox, Darryl Zanuck made a great deal of money off Betty Grable, but left to his own devices, he preferred sexy brunettes: Gene Tierney, Linda Darnell, Jean Peters.

As for Paramount, they managed to luck out for years by what amounted to a lack of definition. If you can discern any pattern at all in Paramount's leading ladies, you're a better man than I, Gunga Din.

For a long time, Marlene Dietrich was the studio's signature actress. She was hired as a Garbo competitor and proved to be more adaptable and far hardier in the bargain; for one thing, she had a more approachable brand of sexuality; for another, she had genuine humor.

Paramount's major discovery in the last half of the 1930s was Dorothy Lamour; their big star during World War II besides Betty Hutton was Veronica Lake, who didn't last long, for reasons that had little to do with talent. Lake was very difficult, had problems with alcohol, and was given to anti-Semitic outbursts. Otherwise, she was a sweetheart.

RKO and Columbia, the studios that stood near the bottom of the list of majors, were rarely able to gather enough top talent to have a particular style or approach to actresses. RKO had Ginger Rogers for a number of years, and they did very well for each other, while Columbia had Jean Arthur, and ditto. But there was never a sense of actorly identity at those studios, largely, I believe, because neither was run by people with a bent for long-term thinking, which was quite the reverse at MGM and Warners, which consciously built their operations to last.

Ginger started out as a gum-cracking chorus girl, but revealed her inner swan when she was paired with Fred Astaire in *Flying Down to Rio*. They made nine more movies together. Forests have been felled trying to explain their particular chemistry. Simply put, they looked—and danced—as if they belonged together, as if they hadn't been matched up by a movie studio, but by God. When Astaire and Rogers were in motion, they had the easy camaraderie of a couple that had met in grade school and had had an understanding ever since.

That amity didn't always extend to their relationship offscreen. Fred and Ginger dated briefly in New York before the movies called, but there hadn't been anything in particular between them. In later years Fred could be a little grumpy about Ginger, and he wasn't crazy about her mother, who was omnipresent. He was very funny about Ginger's penchant for scene-stealing costumes. He felt such gestures were self-defeating and rather silly, because they took attention away from the dancer's body, which was, after all, the point.

But he never said a word against her work ethic or her skills as a dancer. Nor could he, because the basis for their shared magic was their dancing. One critic noted that they seldom kiss in their movies, but they don't have to—their sex life takes place when they dance, and those scenes are among the most rapturously convincing love scenes ever filmed.

That Fred and Ginger respected each other as professionals more than they loved each other as man and woman is a testament to the strange alchemy of performance. People talk about the magic of the movies, but there's also a mystery to them, and it's personified by Astaire and Rogers.

As the 1930s were ending, Fox was unleashing a new queen of the studio: Betty Grable. She was born in St. Louis but came to Hollywood at an early age, where she graduated from the Hollywood Professional School. After that, Betty went to work in the chorus. You can see her as the third girl on the left in Goldwyn musicals with Eddie Cantor, such as *Palmy Days*.

A few years later, she was getting leads in RKO B movies, and then Darryl Zanuck brought her to Fox as a means of keeping Alice Faye in line. (Alice and Darryl heartily disliked each other, but then Alice wasn't all that crazy about show business in the first place.) I seriously doubt that Darryl had any idea that Betty would become as huge a star as she did.

When Alice had to have some minor surgery, rather than wait a month to start a picture called *Down Argentine Way*, Darryl simply substituted Betty as the star. The picture turned out to be a huge hit. Most Fox musicals were, but they were never as ambitious as the musicals Arthur Freed made at MGM. That just might have been the reason the Fox vehicles were so reliable—with the exception of the Mickey and Judy shows, MGM musicals were rarely the same, while the Fox musicals were heavily patterned. If you liked one, you'd like them all. Even the titles had a geographically similar bent: *Down Argentine Way*, *Tin Pan Alley*, *Moon Over Miami*, *Springtime in the Rockies*, and so on.

Two things worked in Betty's favor: Technicolor and World War II. The former showcased her luscious peaches-and-cream complexion, and the latter made Betty into the pinup of pinups. Besides that, her sunny personality was a perfect respite for wartime audiences. Harry Brand, the head of publicity at Fox, insured Betty's legs for a million dollars, or at least he said he did, and by the end of the war not only was she Fox's highest-paid star, she was the movie industry's, as well.

Betty's films were undemanding and made great amounts of money for the studio. Darryl's only complaint about her was her habit of closing down production for a day to take in a particularly hot horse race. Nobody but a hugely successful movie star could have done such a thing, but Darryl put up with it. I suspect he was actually a little embarrassed by her pictures, as he went out of his way to produce a given number of projects each year that might be termed the anti-Grable movies—startlingly downbeat efforts like *The Ox-Bow Incident* or *Gentleman's Agreement*. He even tried to broaden Betty's own appeal by casting her in a noir drama called *I Wake Up Screaming*, but she seemed uncomfortable with it, and so did the audience—our Betty, menaced by a killer? The only thing that could threaten Betty Grable was falling off her platform shoes.

After World War II, Darryl seemed to sense that Betty's heyday might be passing, so he upgraded her collaborators; he got her a posthumous Gershwin score for *The Shocking Miss Pilgrim*, and he hired Preston Sturges to write and direct a film for her called *The Beautiful Blonde from Bashful Bend*, a Western parody that died the death, and deserved to.

But audiences continued to love her, and justifiably so—she ranked in the top ten box office stars for ten consecutive years, from 1941 to 1951, something no other female star has ever accomplished. (Doris Day placed ten years on the list, but not consecutively.)

As I found out when I got to know Betty, she was a totally sincere and kind person who refused the easy alternative of an ironic view of the world. She was beloved around the studio; the crews adored her because she was one of them—an unpretentious girl who never forgot her days in the chorus. Betty worked hard and liked to have a good time, and people responded in kind.

Even comedians liked Betty. Take Lucille Ball. Comedy was Lucy's profession, not her personality. Lucy wasn't particularly funny offstage, but she appreciated people who were, and she always said that if she needed to laugh she simply spent some time with Betty Grable.

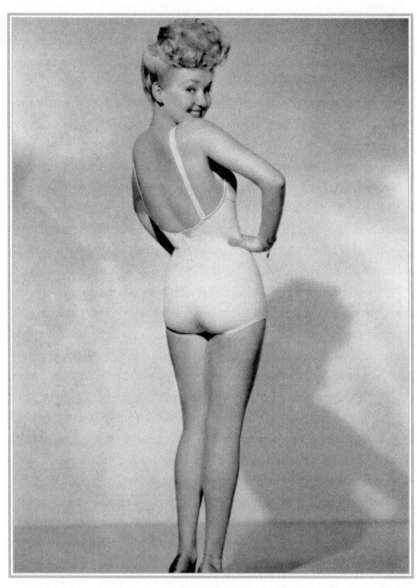

Betty Grable

Betty's film career ended early; she made her last movie in 1955, when she was only thirty-nine—young by modern standards, but Betty was a song-and-dance girl, and the feathers-and-sequins vehicles that were her specialty were heading toward the exit in favor of lavish versions of big Broadway musicals. She was up for the part of Miss Adelaide in the movie version of *Guys and Dolls*, but lost out to Vivian Blaine, who had done it on stage. A hit like that would have propped up Betty for a few years, at least, and given her a second wind. Instead, she kept her hand in doing nightclubs and theater, and she never stopped following the horses.

Her end was unhappy. Her husband, Harry James, was a degenerate gambler and spent most of her money, and then she got cancer. I remember visiting her in the hospital not long before the end; she was very ill, but she still had that bright spirit that endeared her to millions of people all over the world. She wanted her friends as well as her audiences to have a good time. As I sat there with her, I was so moved—she was trying to get me to laugh, trying to make me feel comfortable. This darling woman was only fifty-seven when she died.

"I can sing a little, dance a little, and act a little," she said. "I was just lucky, I guess." Actually, those of us who flocked to Betty's musicals in glorious Technicolor were the lucky ones. And we knew it.

Betty Grable's losing a star role in *Guys and Dolls* is the sort of thing that's part of the business—the factors that determine a career are often just a matter of good breaks and bad breaks.

For instance: Ann Sheridan. Warner Bros. publicity department dubbed her "the Oomph Girl," and yes, she was sexy and all that. But she also had a very real quality on-screen, that of a good-hearted dame, which was her real personality coming through. Ann Sheridan played characters who could dish it out as well as take it. They weren't exactly tough but could be if you pushed them too far.

Ann was born Clara Lou Sheridan in Nowheresville, Texas, but she won a beauty contest and made it to Hollywood by the time she was eighteen. She was beautiful, but needed something to break her out of the pack of the ten thousand other girls who were beautiful, too.

Ann told me that it was a Warners' publicist named Bob Taplinger who had George Hurrell take some photos of her that reeked of sex. He posed her in a silk robe that was provocatively sliding off her shoulder and with rumpled hair, as if she'd just gotten out of a very active bed. There was nothing overt in the image, but the lighting and the look in her eyes told you everything you needed to know.

Those photographs changed everything for Annie. Before that, she'd been just one of the girls playing throwaway parts, but now she started getting real roles in real movies (*Angels with Dirty Faces*, *City for Conquest*, *Kings Row*). Despite this, the studio's attitude toward her never changed; Warners was a Darwinian environment where only the strong and the loud survived. Ironically, Ann was never cast as the sexpot the Hurrell stills implied.

"I had to fight for everything at Warners," Ann once told me. "Everybody had to fight. Cagney, Davis, Flynn, everybody. A knockdown, drag-out fight." Ann spent a lot of years at the studio at a time when it was very difficult to be a female star there.

Bette Davis was in uncontested first position, and then came Joan Crawford. Olivia de Havilland was there for years as well, which left actresses like Ida Lupino and Ann struggling simply because the premiere scripts were always going to be earmarked for the biggest stars.

In 1947, Ann left Warners, and it looked like things were going to be fine. She signed for *Good Sam* opposite Gary Cooper and director Leo McCarey, and that was followed by *I Was a Male War Bride* with Cary Grant and Howard Hawks. Marion Marshall, who would become my second wife and the mother of my daughter Kate, was in the latter picture, and had nothing but good things to say about Ann. But *Good Sam* was a flop, and *I Was a Male War Bride* did nothing for her because all anybody talked about was Cary Grant in drag, an image that

Ann Sheridan

was so hilarious and overwhelming that no one even noticed that Ann was in the picture.

After that, she couldn't command A-list projects and went from studio to studio, appearing in films of gradually diminishing importance and budget. And there was another factor: Annie was a hard-drinking, hard-living woman, and the effects of the scotch began to show on her face when she was still young. She was doing a TV series when she died of cancer in 1967 at the age of fifty-two. What a loss—a great lady.

Throughout all this, Ann was a well-liked woman. But she couldn't catch a break when she needed one—she never nabbed the Margo Channing part that would make people sit up and take notice, or even a TV series that would lead to a reassessment of her career. Look at what *I Love Lucy* did for Lucille Ball after a midrange movie career that came to a screeching halt when MGM tried to make her a glamour-puss when she was really a clown.

Ann needed some luck, but didn't get any.

There were any number of other actresses whose careers were not as successful as they should have been. On some level, their expectations weren't met, and many of them closed down a little—or a lot. Acting became the equivalent of a love affair that ended badly—a source of disgruntlement and dissatisfaction.

I didn't know Lauren Bacall terribly well. Spencer Tracy took me to Bogart's house once before Bogie died, and a year or so after Bogie's death Bacall was heavily involved with Frank Sinatra, who was close to Natalie and me. Frank lavished Betty with all of his immense charm and generosity. After nursing Bogie through a dismal cancer that took more than a year to kill him, Betty was in desperate need of positive reinforcement, and Frank supplied all that and more.

Frank had been a good friend of Bogie's, and had really admired him. Somehow or other, Betty assumed that they were going to get married, and the story leaked out. Frank thought the information came from Betty, and he cut her off, which rocked her.

A few years later, Betty married Jason Robards Jr., who resembled Bogie and was like him in another way—Jason was his own man and didn't care overmuch what anybody else thought of him. He also drank even more than Bogie, and that's saying something. The marriage turned into a nonstop battle fueled by Jason's drinking. (He later dried out.)

I used to go surf fishing with Jason. He was a hell of an actor, devoted to his profession, and a good guy . . . when he was sober. The contentious atmosphere bred by drinking attracts me not at all; I don't want to be around it, let alone in it, so I grew slightly apart from Betty when she was married to Jason.

After they divorced, she never remarried, although there were a few long-term relationships. She had a couple of successful Broadway shows and wrote a good memoir, although her movie career remained a sometime thing. In later years, whenever I saw her, there was a sharpness to her, an undertone of bitterness. I don't know if it was her inability to find an equivalently happy relationship with anybody else after Bogie died, professional frustration, or both.

But in the years when we saw each other regularly, I liked Betty a lot. She stood firm, she let you know what she thought, and you ignored her at your peril.

I think it's important to note here how isolated actresses were at this point in the 1940s. As I mentioned, at this time there was precisely one woman director in the business: Dorothy Arzner, and she didn't have a lengthy career—only fifteen years or so. All the studio heads were men, and, with the exception of my friend Minna Wallis, the vast majority of the agents were men as well.

There were precisely three women producers: Harriet Parsons at RKO, Joan Harrison at Universal, and Virginia Van Upp at Columbia.

Harriet was the daughter of Louella Parsons, so everybody figured her position was a patronage job, although if you look at her credits, it's clearly an unfair charge. Joan Harrison had worked with Alfred Hitchcock for years, cowriting the script for *Rebecca* and some other pictures, and was certainly a talent. Years later, Hitchcock would hire her to oversee his TV show, *Alfred Hitchcock Presents,* which she ran like a Swiss watch for ten years. After that, she married the novelist Eric Ambler and retired to England. As for Virginia Van Upp, she was Harry Cohn's right-hand woman and produced *Gilda,* among other movies.

Add to that reality the fact that most women's starring careers were quite short. Men could go on playing leads until decrepitude, but for actresses, turning forty was typically a death knell for leading parts. It had been that way since the silent days for reasons both technical—the early film stock tended toward the harsh and was merciless on even minor signs of aging—and cultural.

It seems to me that women were also regarded in a more overtly sexual way than men were. Bogart, Cagney, and Wayne were never typical romantic leading men, so they could age. Nobody thought anything of it unless their screen pairings verged on the absurd, such as Bogart and Gary Cooper both taking a run at a dewy Audrey Hepburn in *Sabrina* and *Love in the Afternoon.* Bogie and Coop may have only been old enough to be her father, but they looked old enough to be her grandfather.

Women had a much narrower window of opportunity. Actresses as varied as Miriam Hopkins, Kay Francis, and Norma Shearer all saw their careers decline either just before they hit forty or just after. Cases such as Claudette Colbert and Bette Davis, who sailed on into middle age and beyond, have always been the exceptions.

Actresses with any degree of self-awareness know the clock is ticking, and it lights the fire of urgency in many of them to get as much work as they can as soon as they can, if only because nothing's as cold as the movie business when you're considered passé.

Women also faced financial hurdles. Jimmy Stewart got a percentage of the profits as early as 1950; a woman wasn't granted that until Elizabeth Taylor and *Cleopatra*, more than ten years later. Men were in control, and women had to fight just to stay even. A woman like Barbara Stanwyck was strong, and had to be; otherwise, she would never have been able to flourish for as long as she did.

In order to gain leverage within the industry in which they worked, actresses dealt with the situation in different ways. Some, like Irene Dunne or Claudette Colbert, would be ladylike but very firm—Colbert's shooting day ended at 5 P.M. and not a minute later. Joan Crawford would often sleep with her director. Bette Davis could be a holy terror, and since most men try to avoid angry women, they would give her de facto control as a means of placating her. John Huston stated the truth: "The studio was afraid of her."

What made Bette mad? Mainly, deceiving her or lying to her. But on a deeper level, almost everything, up to and including the fact of being under contract to a studio. As Bette once told me, "I could be forced to do anything the studio told me to do. They could ask a contract player to appear in a burlesque house. The only recourse was to refuse, and then you were suspended without pay. When you were under suspension, without salary, you couldn't work in a Woolworth's. You could only starve."

Actually, she omitted one detail: The length of time you were suspended was added to the back end of your contract.

In essence, being under contract meant that the studio owned you and could do as it wished with you. From the studio's point of view, the appropriate response of its employees should have been "Be grateful and shut up." They had taken nobodies and made them into somebodies, and those nobodies had been exposed to no financial risk whatsoever in the process. But from Bette's point of view, the terms of the deal amounted to servitude, and the very fact of it was an abiding irritant.

Not everybody felt as vehemently as she did; for some, who were born in a small town or had spent years struggling in vaudeville or the theater, signing a contract with a studio felt like a perfectly fair exchange in return for a great deal of money and job security.

Of course, such security was only temporary. When MGM was thinking of dumping Joan Crawford, they put her in something called *The Ice Follies of 1939,* which was one way to scrawl the handwriting on the wall. She recouped somewhat when they cast her in *The Women,* and *A Woman's Face* is certainly a strong movie, but she was still gone from MGM by 1943.

The nature of the transaction was very clear. As Clark Gable characterized it, "I am paid not to think . . . and to be obedient."

Some actresses fought back legally. Bette and Olivia de Havilland both dragged Jack Warner into court. Olivia worked for him from 1935 to 1943, and when her contract expired she decided to go out on her own. Then Warner informed her that she owed the studio another six months because of the time she had been on suspension for refusing parts. Olivia sued and Olivia won. The ruling that found in her favor improved conditions for actors and actresses alike.

After doing battle with carnivores like Jack Warner or Harry Cohn six days a week, how could you go home and quietly mix a drink for yourself and your husband? These guys were killers, and to work for them on a continuing basis you had to be as overbearing as they were just to stay even. But the dance was a difficult one to manage—if an actress wasn't tough, she wouldn't survive, but she couldn't let too much of that toughness show on-screen, or it could be off-putting to the audience, not to mention to her leading man. People make jokes about Joan Crawford's shoulder pads and a demeanor that got more imperious with each passing year, but you can see all that as the price of doing business.

I've mentioned something else that comes into play with careers, and that is luck. Breaks. When they land in front of you, you have to take advantage of them, but they have to land there first.

Bogart only got *The Maltese Falcon* because George Raft turned it down—he didn't want to work with a first-time director, who happened to be John Huston. As a matter of fact, George Raft made several careers because of his insensitivity to good scripts—he also turned down *Double Indemnity,* so Fred MacMurray got to actor's heaven.

So much of it is fortune; so much of it is breaks.

All of us bring ourselves to the screen; somehow or another the soul, the loving essence of a person, usually comes through the lens of the camera and resides in the film. I've mentioned how Bette Davis emphasized her character's passion and irascibility in *All About Eve*. Bette was drawn to those aspects of the character—the jealousy, the blood on the show-business floor—because that's the way she perceived her life and career: as a constant struggle.

When she was a young actress in New York, she was denied admission to the Civic Repertory Theatre by the great Eva Le Gallienne; when she got a job in a stock company in Rochester, she was fired by the director, a young George Cukor. Her first screen test, for Sam Goldwyn, was rejected. When she was finally signed for the movies, by Universal, Carl Laemmle famously said that she had about as much sex appeal as the gangly comic Slim Summerville, and she was quickly thrown overboard.

It wasn't that she didn't have talent, it was her looks and her inability to project the simpering adoration of the leading man that was expected of young leading ladies of that period. She simply was not a conventional ingénue by any means, and she never simpered. And then there was the larger fact that she had a tendency to want to do things her own way, theatrical courtesies be damned.

She was saved by George Arliss, speaking of unconventional-looking actors. Arliss looked a lot like a fish, and he appears remarkably hammy to modern eyes, but his thundering style earned a great deal of respect back in the day. When he hired Bette to make *The Man Who Played God* with him, and then went out of his way to praise her abilities, it got a lot of people's attention and earned her a contract at Warner Bros.

The thing to remember about Bette was that all the rejection she endured only strengthened her desire to make it. Her attitude was never "Maybe they're right . . .," it was "I'll show those ignorant bastards!"

She regarded Jack Warner as the primary ignorant bastard, simply because Jack was congenitally disinclined to believe anything an actor ever told him. It took him years to figure out what to do with Bette, but through sheer bloody-minded perseverance she gradually accrued the outlines of a screen character—a woman who would do as she pleased, consequences be damned.

By 1944, when I was going to the movies several times a week, Bette was a huge star, with movies like *Jezebel, Dark Victory, The Letter, The Little Foxes, Mr. Skeffington,* and *Now, Voyager.* A couple of them were great, but all of them were unforgettable, simply because of Bette's strength and a personality so forceful you couldn't take your eyes off her, even when she was playing a bedraggled caterpillar who was soon to become a beautiful butterfly in *Now, Voyager.*

Bette had a magnificent instrument, magnificent body behavior. She was a small woman, but she came into the movie frame with a rush, as if she owned the light and couldn't wait for the arcs to warm her face. She took a scene and ran with it. That's the way she saw the work, and that's the way she saw life—as a battle to be won, and she was determined to vanquish anyone or anything that got in between her and what she believed to be the truth of a character or a script. And if there weren't any obstacles, Bette was quite capable of creating them, just so she could sail into battle.

She wanted to dominate, which is why she married weak men. Her husbands were, in order, Harmon Nelson, Arthur Farnsworth, William Grant Sherry, and Gary Merrill. Well, Gary Merrill wasn't actually weak, as he gave Bette as good as he got, but most of it was the booze talking, and that only inflamed the situation. You couldn't win with Bette in a romantic relationship.

Professionally or personally, she didn't want to be told what to do. She bridled at William Wyler, who insisted in sculpting her performances in *Jezebel, The Letter,* and *The Little Foxes.* She was attracted to

Bette Davis

the *idea* of strength in a man—she and Wyler had a brief affair—but she would not, could not be subservient, not even to a director as great as Wyler, with whom, I believe, she did her best work. She could overwhelm a weak director and battle a strong one to the point of mutual exhaustion.

I first met Bette just about the time she was doing *All About Eve* through our mutual friend Claire Trevor. We were at Claire's house in Newport Beach. Bette and I became good friends and stayed good friends for the rest of her life. I produced *Madame Sin*, a TV movie that Bette starred in, and got to witness her firsthand as a destructive force. She gave David Greene, the director, a very hard time, but he deserved it—he lied to her, and you could not lie to Bette.

What always surprised people about Bette was the extent of her domesticity. She took her work quite seriously, but that was also true of her private time. She loved to cook New England boiled dinners—lobster and such—and that alone set her off from almost all the actresses who were her contemporaries. It's not that none of them could cook, it's that they worked six days a week. On the seventh day, they needed to rest, and their homes were not staging areas for parties so much as they were a refuge, a retreat from the exhausting pressures of show business.

Bette would rent in places like Laguna, and they were always lovely houses—I particularly remember one she had in Coldwater Canyon. Whether she owned or rented, she had a housekeeper who traveled with her and kept her homes the way Bette wanted them kept.

In that era, actors were itinerant and grew used to living in hotels, so they didn't really have much opportunity to develop a decorating taste of their own. When the serious money started rolling in, decorators became necessary; they could help stars find the proper style that would set them off. In the process of seeing what other women were doing with their houses, and in hiring and firing decorators, actresses could develop a taste of their own.

But even there Bette set her own course. She didn't pay any attention to designers because she knew exactly what she wanted. She had a knack for decorating in a specific style—again, very New England. She would repurpose old wooden commodes for use as end tables. And once you got over the initial surprise—and hesitation—of seeing them, they looked marvelous, if eccentric, and functioned beautifully.

Similarly, Bette was also a good, attentive mother. The children of many stars were raised by nannies, simply because the parents had other priorities—their careers, mainly. But Bette would vacation with her kids, made them not just a part of her life, but a focus of it.

In 1961, she did the original Broadway production of Tennessee Williams's *The Night of the Iguana*, and pulled the play down around her head like Samson bringing down the temple. She didn't act the part. Instead, she turned a perfectly good script into "The Bette Davis Show." She wouldn't take direction and she antagonized her leading man to the point that he tried to strangle her during a rehearsal.

When she made her entrance on opening night, she was greeted by an ovation, and she responded by breaking character, walking down to the edge of the stage, and clasping her hands over her head like a triumphant prizefighter. The crowd ate it up, but her behavior was completely disrespectful of the play and her fellow actors.

All this derived from fear. Her marriage to Gary Merrill had just broken up, she was drinking too much, her movie career was in the doldrums, and she was losing her looks. She was desperate for the love of the audience. Tennessee Williams was equally desperate for a hit, which was the only reason he didn't fire her. And Bette did sell tickets, although what the audience saw wasn't *The Night of the Iguana*, but something else entirely.

The reviews were pretty bad, and Bette blamed Tennessee, blamed the director, blamed everyone but herself. Classic self-sabotage.

Tennessee certainly had his problems, but *The Night of the Iguana* had good bones—strong characters clashing in interesting ways. Bette left after 128 performances, and the show struggled on for a while longer. The play was converted into a fine movie by John Huston. Because of the stellar cast, it's probably a better film than it was a play, but it could still have provided Bette with a springboard. Instead, *The Night of the Iguana* was regarded as a flamboyant flop. Neurosis is usually a component of failure, but there are ways that neurosis can be converted into strength. When Bette was thirty, she knew that; when she was fifty-six, she had forgotten it.

For all of her volatility and the special handling she mandated, I always adored her. Her personal courage never flagged. She brought up a mentally disabled daughter, which was extraordinarily difficult emotionally. She did the best job she could raising her children, and I genuinely believe that the vile memoir her daughter B.D. wrote helped kill her—it was the kind of primal betrayal that destroys the will to live.

Bette spoke to me about the book. She wasn't so much angry as broken by it. I had heard B.D. tell her that she was the greatest mother in the world, that only Bette would have stuck with her through thick and thin. And then to have the child you thought loved you betray you, not just privately but publicly . . .

At first Bette couldn't believe it was happening; later she tried to avoid talking about it. It was the worst thing that ever happened to her; it was the worst thing that ever could have happened to her. She never got over it, and the people who loved Bette never got over it, either.

When Bette died in 1989, she was buried at Forest Lawn in the Hollywood Hills, looking down on the Warner Bros. lot in Burbank, where she had worked for more than fourteen years. Robert Osborne and Kathy Sermak, Bette's loyal assistant and surrogate daughter, planned the memorial service on Stage 18 at Warners, Bette's favorite stage. She had made *The Letter*, *Old Acquaintance*, and *Now, Voyager* there, among others. She used to say that the reason she liked Warners as much as she did was because it was a "workers" studio. She would have gone crazy at MGM, with Norma Shearer and Greer Garson swanning around.

The atmosphere on Stage 18 was that of a film set. There were lights, there were cameras, there were film props, including the clock that had been on the set of *Mr. Skeffington*. Above the podium was a screen to project film clips. On either side of the screen, enormous photographs of Bette hung by thin wires strung from the rafters.

People who had loved and respected Bette were there: Clint Eastwood, George Hamilton, Vincent Price, Stefanie Powers, Glenn Ford, Diane Baker, Teresa Wright. Jill and I were there, of course, and the contingent from the Warner Bros. of Bette's era included the screenwriter Julius Epstein, the director Vincent Sherman, the editor Rudi Fehr, and the actress Joan Leslie.

The hosts were David Hartman, James Woods, and Angela Lansbury. Jimmy Woods said that seeing Bette in *Now, Voyager* had inspired him to pursue an acting career, and that Bette wrote a poetry on the screen that was the equal of Yeats: "There are two kinds of people, those of us who write poetry and those of us who read it. Even those of us who couldn't read poetry, read her work with some amount of genius, simply because of the beauty with which she'd written it." After the remembrances and the film clips, Bette's own version of "I Wish You Love" was played, and then I got up and turned on the work light, which is the signal on a film set that the day's work is done and it's time to go home.

As we filed out, each of us was given a white rose as a memento of one of the most remarkable human beings we had ever known.

Later, Kathy Sermak gave me a pewter ashtray with an oak handle that Bette had always carried with her while she smoked and prowled through her house. That battered ashtray and Bette's friendship will always be two of my most prized possessions.

Bette brought passion to her work, but an actress like Rosalind Russell brought something else: joy. Roz had a most interesting career; she was never one of the hot, sexy young actresses of the moment. She was good-looking, but no more than that. What she had was an incandescent gift for comedy. (I wasn't crazy about Roz in drama—like Norma Shearer, she tended to go for noble uplift, and that killed her natural ebullience.)

Roz was another New England girl, born in Connecticut to a lawyer and a fashion editor, who sent their daughter to the American Academy of Dramatic Arts.

Because Roz grew up in a two-career house, she was very comfortable playing women who had no intention of devoting their lives to a man, or even conceding a point. But it took her a while to find her sea legs. She was making movies as early as 1934, and you can see the filmmakers trying to figure out what would work for this high-energy but not overwhelmingly beautiful girl.

She started to hit her stride in 1935, when she made *China Seas* opposite heavyweights Clark Gable and Jean Harlow and more than held her own. Her career hit fourth gear with comedies like *The Women* and *Four's a Crowd*, and she alternated comedy with drama for the rest of her career.

To watch Roz in pictures like *His Girl Friday* and *Auntie Mame* is to see a woman who can do both near-slapstick and stylized high comedy. She had energy, and she had timing that was spot on. Cary Grant made everyone who worked with him look good, but Roz made Cary even better than he was ordinarily, because she gave him confidence— whatever he threw at her, she could return. If you stuck to the script, Roz could give the words a twist or lilt that made the lines seem better than they were; if you wanted to improvise, Roz could hit the ball back over the net with ease.

Yet Roz was wildly underrated in her time, largely, I think, because she was a talent in a time that was largely devoted to beauty. Even now, she's not spoken of as one of the greats, although I think she was, and her best pictures are in constant rotation on Turner Classic Movies.

I got to know Roz in the 1950s, when Natalie and I lived down the street from her. A few years later, Natalie worked with her in *Gypsy*. We both thought Roz was subtly miscast as Momma Rose, a part that Natalie and I felt cried out for Judy Garland. But Jack Warner refused even to

Rosalind Russell

consider hiring Judy because he felt she had personally driven the budget of *A Star Is Born* to outlandish heights—she simply refused to show up on time, day after day, week after week. That, and the fact that she and Sid Luft, her hustler/husband, had stolen furniture from the studio and used it to furnish their house.

Roz could Rex Harrison her way through a song, but by the time she came to make *Gypsy,* her voice had gotten very deep and throaty from age and cigarettes, narrowing what little range she had. A lot of her songs had to be dubbed, and rather obviously so.

As a woman, Roz was very tasteful and quite religious, although not relentlessly pious in the way that Loretta Young was. Mostly, Roz was perpetually *involved*—she always had a project or six. Like Claire Trevor, she had an innately positive outlook on life.

When Roz threw a dinner party, everything was impeccable. The food and wine, of course, but also the guest list. Cary Grant would be there, especially when he was married to Barbara Hutton, with whom Roz was very close. Barbara once gave Roz a stunning piece of jewelry, a gorgeous bracelet that was white gold and baguettes. But when Roz named her newborn son Lance, Barbara saw red, because she had also named *her* son Lance—a name she had gotten out of a Victorian novel.

Barbara felt that Roz had violated some sort of personal copyright she held on the name Lance and stopped speaking to her old friend. The extremely close friendship was over. Small-world department: Years later, Barbara's son, Lance, married Jill St. John. Barbara adored him all his life, until his tragic death in a plane crash.

(Speaking of jewelry, the owner of what might have been the finest jewelry collection in Hollywood was Sonja Henie, although there are those who think Paulette Goddard's was even better, and I often heard Merle Oberon's name mentioned in that regard, as well. Why Paulette and Sonja Henie? I think it might be because they were more involved with the gifts they received from their lovers and husbands than they were with their lovers and husbands. Jewelry *mattered* to them—it was a way of keeping score. After Henie's movie career was over, she fronted an ice show that was quite lucrative, and she remained attentive to the kind of men who were, shall we say, generous by nature.)

Everyone liked Roz. Nobody liked her husband, Freddie Brisson, who was known to everybody in Hollywood as "The Lizard of Roz." Freddie was universally disliked because—how to put this delicately?—because he was an arrogant asshole.

Nobody could ever figure out from where Freddie's arrogance derived, because he really hadn't accomplished much. He was the son of Carl Brisson, an actor who had starred in one of Hitchcock's early movies, *The Ring*, in 1927. Freddie produced some of Roz's pictures and some of Roz's plays, but like a lot of Hollywood mates he was basically a satellite that orbited the star's planet. But that reflected glory was enough to give Freddie a head the size of Jupiter.

Everyone put up with Freddie because, well, Roz was Roz.

And they did have a great backstory: Freddie was Danish and had sailed to America in late 1939. The trip across the Atlantic took about twelve days, because the ship had to keep zigzagging to avoid German U-boats. The passengers on the boat only had two movies to keep them amused. One of them was *The Women*, which featured Roz. Freddie fell in love with her through the movie.

When he got to New York, he sent a telegram to Cary Grant, who was a friend from his days in England. Cary responded by inviting Freddie to Hollywood and told him that he would be happy to introduce Freddie to Miss Russell, with whom he just happened to be costarring in *His Girl Friday*.

Freddie got to Hollywood, and went to Chasen's at a prearranged time. Cary showed up with Roz, but she didn't understand what was happening—she thought she was on a date with Cary. Freddie persisted and got her phone number anyway, then pursued her for weeks before it finally dawned on her that Cary wasn't interested, but that Freddie was.

When they got married in 1941, Cary was best man, and when Roz died in 1976, Cary was a pallbearer.

True story.

By this point you might be noticing the emergence of a theme here—strong women marrying weak or inappropriate men. There were dozens of examples of this in the Hollywood I grew up in, and I'm sure there are dozens more in modern Hollywood. Sometimes you can figure out what impels a woman to choose one man over another; other times it's a complete mystery.

Laraine Day had a solid career in the late 1930s and 1940s, starting out in the Dr. Kildare series at MGM and graduating to name-above-the-title status in movies like Hitchcock's *Foreign Correspondent*, *The Locket*, and *Mr. Lucky* with Cary Grant. Laraine was regarded as a very pleasant woman, so everybody was stunned when she married Leo Durocher, the manager of the Brooklyn and Los Angeles Dodgers, and the man who voiced the phrase "Nice guys finish last."

I knew Leo quite well—too well. Leo loved the nightlife, loved to gamble, and he loved women, whether he was married to them or not. The strange thing about their marriage was that Laraine was a Mormon, and if you were going to choose a group of characteristics least likely to appeal to a Mormon, every one of them would have been embodied by Leo.

One day Leo asked me to lend him $10,000. I didn't ask him what it was for, but I imagine it was for a gambling debt he didn't want Laraine to know about. I gave him the money.

Six months later, I was still waiting for my money. A few months after that I went to Frank Sinatra, who had a lot more experience in loaning large amounts than I did.

I told Frank my tale of woe and was met with a shrug. "When you hand a man that kind of money," Frank told me, "be prepared to kiss it good-bye. That's the way it is."

I appreciated his point, but $10,000 meant a lot more to me than it did to Frank. I had to put quite a lot of pressure on Leo, and for quite a long time, but he did eventually repay me.

I can't say I was surprised when Leo and Laraine divorced. I learned a lesson, and I imagine Laraine did as well.

But back to Roz.

Buoyant, smart, the life of every party, she maintained her joie de vivre in spite of professional dry spells and, later, bad health. When her movie career began to decline in the early 1950s, she took a part in the national tour of John Van Druten's play *Bell, Book and Candle*. Movie stars might do a play in New York, but with the exception of Henry Fonda, they didn't tour with them. But Roz got great reviews, which led to her being cast in the Leonard Bernstein show *Wonderful Town*, which in turn led to her creating the role of Auntie Mame in 1956, which was followed by the movie.

Roz was up for anything, and I loved that about her. She was interested in politics—Roz was a moderate Republican, a fan of Eisenhower's—was a great baseball fan, following the Dodgers religiously, first when they were in Brooklyn, more so after they moved to Los Angeles. She even had season tickets.

She excelled at playing madcap characters, even though she was actually a deeply sensible person. At Christmas, she would have a group of friends over for a big Scandinavian meal—a gesture to Freddie. Each guest would be given a paper bag filled with costume jewelry, ribbons, and some straight pins. The lights would be turned off, some candles would be lit, and everyone would have the task of making some kind of hat out of the items in their bag.

When the lights were turned on, there would be Jimmy Stewart or Gary Cooper wearing a goofy creation on his head.

Roz got cancer in the early 1960s and had a mastectomy. After that came a bad case of rheumatoid arthritis. The steroids she took to alleviate the discomfort caused her to puff up. It affected her looks but also seemed to slow her down emotionally. She made her last picture in 1971, a not very good movie called *Mrs. Pollifax–Spy* that she wrote herself. Roz died five years later, and I served along with Cary Grant as a pallbearer. It was something I was happy to do for one of the brightest lights of Hollywood, as well as one of the great ladies of show business.

One of the prime differences between the actresses of that generation and the modern variety was their sense of the grand manner—they lived high and they lived large. They developed entourages that were every bit the equal of those of their male counterparts, but with a subtle difference. The chums of male stars were drinking buddies or pals they could blow off steam with. Errol Flynn was an Aussie—well, technically he was Tasmanian, but close enough—and his pals tended not to be actors or studio people, but stuntmen and various hangers-on. But the people female stars counted on were usually connected with them professionally in some way. I've mentioned, for example, how Barbara Stanwyck depended on Helen Ferguson, her publicist.

Then there were people like Sydney Guilaroff. He was the leading hairdresser to the stars, and he had a clientele that numbered dozens of major actresses as well as professional hostesses. A star's personal hairdresser took precedence over whoever was in charge of that kind of thing at any studio, because they usually brought their core group of support professionals with them—hairdresser, makeup person, and so forth. For the stars, it was a kind of security blanket—they knew that their team had only their best interests at heart and weren't prone to studio politics. Their loyalty was to one person and one person only.

Actresses told Sydney everything. About everybody. Women told him about their husbands, their lovers, because they knew he would never break a confidence. And he never did. Even when he wrote a memoir at the end of his life, he was circumspect; if Sydney had wanted to tell the truth, he could have burned the town down.

I got to know Jennifer Jones in the 1970s, when we did *The Towering Inferno* together. It was her last picture, and I would classify her as . . .

interesting. Personally, Jennifer liked me; I had worked with her son, Robert Walker Jr., and we got along very well. Jennifer appreciated that.

I think she spent her career in terror of her profession. Jennifer's real name was Phylis Isley, and she was the daughter of a prominent movie exhibitor in Oklahoma and Texas. He showed a lot of pictures made by Republic, the B-movie studio where John Wayne spent more than fifteen years. Jennifer wanted to be an actress, and since Republic wanted to keep Phil Isley happy, they were happy to give his daughter a beginner's acting contract for seventy-five dollars a week.

She made a serial, and a couple of Westerns, and before you know it she was picked up by Selznick and Fox, where she made *The Song of Bernadette*. Suddenly this little girl from the Southwest was swimming in very turbulent waters. It wasn't easy for her.

Jennifer had a trusting, childlike quality. I was told that the great director King Vidor figured out that to get her in the proper place for the work on *Duel in the Sun*, he had to begin each morning by telling her the story of the movie right up to the scenes they were going to shoot that day. Each day's shooting was a piece of a jigsaw puzzle, and Jennifer needed to know precisely which piece of the puzzle she was doing. At that stage in her life, her self-image was not that of a professional actress but of a little girl who was in far over her head. Being invited to Jennifer's was like going to a hospital ward. For one thing, she would be late for her own dinner. Not ten minutes, but an hour or an hour and a half. She was into Reichian therapy at that point.

I don't honestly know if she ever got over her fears. Years before I got to know Jennifer, I had watched her perform a scene from *Love Is a Many-Splendored Thing* at the Fox studio. I noticed that the hem of her dress was fluttering because her knees were shaking so badly. Off to the side of the set, you could see her then-husband, David Selznick, hovering, watching his wife protectively. Bill Holden, her costar, was fond of her, but he couldn't help but be aware of her anxiety.

She was very much the star, and at the same time she had an intense need for emotional security. Selznick's death in 1965 left her unmoored

Jennifer Jones

for a long time. Contrary to the general opinion that Selznick smothered her, I think David gave her the protection that was absolutely necessary if she was to function at anything approaching a high level.

David had an exaggerated personality; Elia Kazan told me a story that illustrates just how exaggerated. Gadge (Kazan's nickname) once went to Selznick's home on Tower Road to talk about a project. The setting couldn't have been more impressive; the house was stunning, the servants both officious and obsequious.

After Kazan was ushered into the house, the head butler turned to one of the lesser minions and said, "Mr. Kazan to see Mr. Selznick." (Who else would Mr. Kazan have been there to see?) The minion went away to announce Gadge to Selznick. From behind a door, Kazan heard Selznick order, "Turn on the fountain!" Kazan entered, and there was David, with the fountain pumping splendidly in the background. The picture was now complete.

You get that sense of theatrical pomp in most of David's movies, splendid as they were and are. But David's personality, which was directly replicated in his films, belonged to an earlier time in Hollywood; his ornate style couldn't really adapt itself to an environment attuned to acting that was less than grand, or values that were more down market than *Gone with the Wind* or *Since You Went Away*. The great movies of the 1950s—I'm thinking of *High Noon, On the Waterfront, From Here to Eternity, Marty, The Sweet Smell of Success, The Searchers*—couldn't have been made by David if you'd held a gun to his head. He might have appreciated them, but he would never have wanted to spend a year or two of his life making them.

So David and Jennifer were gradually marooned on an island of their own choosing, of the grand and glorious old Hollywood.

Another of the women of this era I knew and grew fond of was Ida Lupino. Ida was actually English, and came from a notable performing family. Her uncle, Lupino Lane, was a very successful comedian in the music halls and West End, as was her dad, Stanley Lupino. Ida's godfather was Ivor Novello, the composer and matinee idol who wrote "Keep the Home Fires Burning" during World War I.

Ida came to Hollywood in the 1930s, but didn't spend all that much time with the British colony. She grew close to David Niven, but then everybody did, because that's the kind of person David was.

She made a big impression in Bill Wellman's *The Light That Failed*. Wellman and star Ronald Colman disliked each other from the first day of production—Colman had wanted a different actress to play opposite him, and when Wellman got his way in casting Ida, Colman made his displeasure known. Ida was left pretty much alone, and responded by sculpting a very dynamic portrayal.

Soon afterward, she went to Warner Bros., where she started off with a big hit: *They Drive by Night*, a tough Raoul Walsh movie about truck drivers, followed by *High Sierra* with Bogart. Ida had the right temperament for that studio—she was a scrapper—but the timing of her arrival was off. Bette Davis was then the unquestioned reigning leading lady, and Ida had to make do with a lot of scripts that Bette turned down. After Joan Crawford came to the lot, the situation got even worse for Ida.

Ida told me that there was never any open warfare between her and Warners' top actresses. She said that Bette had asked her to play the part of the nasty girl in *The Corn Is Green*, the one who tries to keep the boy in his miserable little town in Wales, but Ida had already been cast in another picture. Ida had a lot of respect for Bette, and would have liked to work with her, but I don't know—the part in *The Corn Is Green* would have been the heavy, opposite Bette's noble schoolteacher. Bette would have wanted a strong actress in the role, so long as there was no question of who was going to be vanquished at the end. Also, Ida might have been too old for the part.

Nevertheless, Ida did get some good roles at Warners—there was *The Sea Wolf*, and she won the New York Film Critics Circle Award for

Ida Lupino

Best Actress for *The Hard Way,* a film she hated making and that not enough people know about even today.

But eventually Ida got tired of always being low woman on the totem pole, so she decided to leave Warners. Jack Warner wanted to sign her up for another seven years, but she wanted out.

"Seven years and no options, Ida. Fifty-two weeks a year," Jack said. "No," said Ida.

Jack immediately slipped into his aggressive mode. "All right, I'm going to tell you something. You'll never act at this studio again." And she never did.

Years later, when Ida directed a couple of TV shows at Warners, she reminded Jack of his vow. "That's directing, not acting," he replied. It was clear that he didn't care about television at all except insofar as it made money for the studio.

After leaving Warners, Ida went over to Fox, where she made *Road House.* She didn't stay there long and she always regretted it; she believed that the great mistake of her acting career was departing Fox at the end of the 1940s. She would go on and on about how much she respected Darryl Zanuck and was in awe of his ability to read every draft of every script, and look not only at the rushes of all the pictures in production, but even at wardrobe tests. People usually say that if they had their life to live over again, they wouldn't change a thing. Not Ida—she always wished she'd stayed with Zanuck.

Ida's prerequisite for a role was that the character she played had to have guts. Straight female leads, girl parts, where the character hovered around waiting for the leading man to do something, she hated. She either refused them or did them badly. Like Bette Davis, she was constitutionally incapable of gazing adoringly at the leading man unless he earned it. Since there are occasions when every actress has to do just that, it was a real limitation on her career. From the things Ida told me, she was well aware of that restraint but wasn't bitter about it.

Instead, she began directing. She would always insist that moving into that role wasn't intentional on her part. She had cowritten a movie with her husband, and it had just started production when the director they had hired had a heart attack. They had to get a substitute and fast, so Ida stepped up. The original director, a gent from the silent days named Elmer Clifton, remained on the set guiding her to keep her from making any mistakes with her setups, so Ida and her husband felt he was entitled to his credit. The picture finished on time, and the reviews were good, so Ida kept directing.

If you look at her movies today, you can see that she was influenced by some of the tough old pros she had worked for, guys like Wellman and Walsh. Ida had already been thinking about directing when she made *High Sierra* for Walsh. She would constantly question him about technical issues—over-the-shoulder shots and eyeline matches, things that Walsh had been doing for so long that it was as automatic as rolling his own cigarette, which I saw him do with one hand.

Ida directed only six pictures, but none of them was bad, and one of them—*The Hitch-Hiker*—was excellent, an unsettling, nasty movie about a psycho on the loose. Ida was very conscious of the fact that she was the only woman director in Hollywood at this time. It was a tenuous position, and she adopted a canny would-you-please-help-me-out attitude toward her all-male crews. I'm not sure this was entirely sincere on Ida's part. She was in all other respects a ballsy woman, not a shrinking violet in any way, but she probably felt it was necessary for her continued survival. The crew is particularly important on a low-budget picture—if they slow down even a little bit, you won't finish on time, and that can be a disaster.

All of Ida's pictures were similar to the movies Darryl Zanuck had been making in the early 1930s at Warners—stories spun off from current events and social problems. *Not Wanted* was about unmarried mothers, *Outrage* dealt with a rape, *The Bigamist* was the story of, well, a bigamist. The spice of the subject matter helped make up for the low budgets.

If *The Hitch-Hiker* had Anthony Mann's or John Sturges's name on it as director, it would have given their careers a big boost, but it didn't really do much for Ida. All of her pictures were low-budget B's, and she couldn't manage to climb out of that particular ghetto.

Ida had the same problem that a lot of independent producers had—the system was set up by the studios for the studios, not the independents. Howard Hughes liked Ida's films and gave her financing and distribution through RKO, but she and her husband had to give up 50 percent of the profits in return. Since Ida's pictures were made for about $150,000 apiece, she couldn't afford big stars, which in turn meant that they got limited playing time, usually in double features. There was a ceiling on the money they could earn. Ida made enough money to keep going, but that was about all.

Except for the fact that her pictures weren't particularly commercial, I've always thought Ida would have been good at running a studio. She was smart and savvy—not the same things, by the way—and had a solid, realistic big-picture sense of the movie industry.

She also had an eye for scripts and an eye for talent; in 1952, she hired an art director named Harry Horner to direct a little movie for RKO. Horner had worked with Max Reinhardt in Europe and done beautiful work on pictures like *The Heiress*, for which he won an Oscar. *Beware, My Lovely*, the movie he did for Ida, was quite good. (Horner was the father of James Horner, the late composer who wrote so many great movie scores, including the Oscar-winning score for James Cameron's *Titanic*.)

I'm sure there was some entrenched prejudice against her as a woman director, not because she was a woman per se, but because she was trying to break into the boys' club. And there was another factor. When Ida started directing, Hollywood was being buffeted by a rapidly diminishing audience. Television was siphoning off a lot of the public, and the low-budget pictures Ida was directing couldn't break through in any large way. The studios began making fewer and fewer B movies, and the ones they were releasing veered toward exploitation pictures from producers like American International. Ida didn't want to do that kind of work. Her company, Filmmakers, tried to distribute its own pictures in order to make more money, but the plan failed and they went out of business. Ida, like a lot of male directors, had to go into TV in order to keep working.

She proved to be more successful in television than she had in movies, and her work was solid. She did all kinds of shows, including some that were by no means earmarked for female directors, as was common at that time. Ida directed episodes of tough, suspense-oriented series like *The Twilight Zone*, *Thriller*, *The Fugitive*, *The Untouchables*, and *Have Gun, Will Travel*, as well as some relationship-based programs.

The interesting thing was that the shows that were actually run by women—Loretta Young, Donna Reed—didn't hire Ida. She couldn't get work that was tagged for female audiences.

I don't think she cared, particularly; she just thought it was ironic.

I always got a subliminal feeling that Ida felt that she had shortchanged her acting career by moving into directing. She directed herself only once, in *The Bigamist*, and she didn't like it. She said that it took all her concentration just to direct, and she couldn't divide her attention between being in front of and behind the camera.

I spent a fair amount of time with Ida in Hawaii, when she was married to Howard Duff. She was a great deal of fun—outgoing and vivacious. She was a middle-aged woman at the time, twelve years older than I was, but I found her very sexy. Nothing happened, but if we'd both been single I suspect it might have. Both Ida and Howard drank pretty heavily when I knew them, and the bottle became a serious problem later in Ida's life.

I worked with Ida on television, in an episode of *It Takes a Thief* in which she was a guest star. Despite the fact that her career had narrowed considerably by then, she came in prepared and was totally professional. Just like the other actresses of her generation, she was demanding about things like wardrobe and camera. It wasn't surprising—they knew that presentation was vital; a bad wardrobe could hurt you, and bad lighting could kill you. It was a trait I would also notice in Bette Davis.

As a movie-struck kid, my favorite actresses were Barbara Stanwyck and Paulette Goddard, for entirely different reasons. I loved Paulette's pictures for Chaplin and DeMille, in which she radiated a healthy sexuality. I was just hitting puberty, and she aroused all sorts of illicit thoughts in my hyperactive teenage mind. But Barbara hit me on the emotional level; when she was acting, she wasn't selling anything, she was just telling the truth.

I've written about Barbara Stanwyck in great detail in *Pieces of My Heart*, and I don't want to repeat myself here. I'll simply say that the relationship that began during the filming of 1953's *Titanic* was one of a handful of transformative experiences in my life. It taught me many things, one of them being how important work was to this generation of actresses. I've mentioned how many of them grew up without fathers or had bad relationships with them, which meant that these young girls and women had usually been the sole support of their families. Work was more than their identity—it meant survival, and that was complicated by the fact that leading ladies in that era had shorter careers than leading men.

That was emphatically the case with Barbara. She loved to work and emotionally she needed to work. She had been very poor as a child and young woman, so money translated into security for her.

Work always improved her mood. When she was preparing for a part, or actually shooting, she would become noticeably more animated. (I confess to having some of these traits myself.) Barbara worked terribly hard on a script. She would memorize all the dialogue, not just her own lines, and she would mentally build an arc for her character, so that she would make emotional as well as dramatic sense as she moved through her scenes. She was an actress who took a specific approach to her craft.

Barbara Stanwyck

Whether it was a movie or TV show didn't seem to make much difference to her; she just wanted to keep acting. And the fact was that, after a certain point, she was no longer offered films, but still got roles on television, which is where the audience that had grown up with her had migrated. Since she loved Westerns, she was quite happy making *The Big Valley*, even though a lot of people thought the show was beneath her. But then almost any TV series would have been beneath Barbara—certainly one of the two or three best film actresses of her time.

Living with someone like Barbara at an early stage in my life made me appreciate the vulnerability of even strong women in a way that would have been impossible had I been associating strictly with younger women.

When you're a kid, you're confident that you'll never fail, you'll never die. But loving Barbara, and knowing some of the older actresses I've talked about, made me realize that people can be crushed, and time and disappointment can make them become something other than their best selves.

One of the big might-have-beens in Barbara's life was losing the female lead in *The Fountainhead*, a picture she very much wanted to do. She had actually taken the property to Henry Blanke at Warner Bros., for whom she had done *My Reputation*. Blanke and she had hit it off, so she wanted to work with him again.

The Fountainhead was set up to star Bogart and Stanwyck until King Vidor was assigned to direct. Vidor had made a lot of great pictures, and Jack Warner gave him a fair amount of authority. Vidor simply didn't think Barbara was sexy enough to play the part of Dominique. This was brutal and it was also unexpected, as Barbara and Vidor had worked together so magnificently on *Stella Dallas* a dozen or so years earlier. Of course, Stella Dallas is a character part, not a sexy role. (It has one of the great endings in movie history, as Stella strides proudly away from her daughter's wedding. With her girl taken care of, Stella's work is done, and she can go on to the next thing.)

Bogart eventually drifted away from *The Fountainhead* and was replaced by Gary Cooper, and on came Patricia Neal to take the female lead. Pat Neal was indeed beautiful, and she was also quite a bit younger than Barbara. Gary and Pat flared up into a huge affair, even though the picture itself wasn't very good.

Barbara's attitude toward all this was philosophical. She didn't like being rejected, of course, but her attitude was "What are you going to do? You have to take these things in stride."

It's an attitude that became my own and has stayed with me all these years. She was right—if we didn't take such setbacks in stride, the streets would quickly fill up with the bodies of actors committing suicide. Every actor or actress who ever lived, every great star, has lost parts he or she would have killed to play. It's the nature of the business.

Barbara taught me that all you can really ask for is your share of at bats. If you get up to the plate enough times, you'll get your hits, and if you're at all lucky, some of them will be home runs. Certainly, that was the case with Barbara; with the possible exception of Kate Hepburn, no actress of her generation is remembered with more affection . . . and respect. I'm no different from anybody else—I have endless respect for her. But I also love her.

How to describe June Allyson to someone who never saw her? She was a little like Meg Ryan in that her appeal was a matter of being young, perky, and approachable. June was really Ella Geisman from the Bronx—another poor kid whose father deserted the family. For emotional sustenance, June went to the movies of Fred Astaire and Ginger Rogers, and got a role in her first film in 1937, when she was only twenty years old.

From there it was on to Broadway, rising in the cast list until she appeared in Cole Porter's *Panama Hattie* in 1940, where she understudied Betty Hutton. When Hutton got sick one night. Allyson went on, and George Abbott realized he had a star in the making—June could sing and dance! Abbott put together *Best Foot Forward* just for June, and that took her to Hollywood.

She was a hit almost immediately in light comedies and musicals like *Good News*, although MGM also used her in occasional dramas like *Little Women*. After that she worked a lot with Jimmy Stewart—*The Stratton Story, The Glenn Miller Story*. In 1955, she appeared in the box office top ten, but after that roles became sparse for June, because tastes started to change and because there was really room for only one perky blonde, and by then that spot was taken by Doris Day.

In my mind, I always bracketed June with Van Johnson. They both became stars during World War II and they had the same sort of image—cute, happy-go-lucky, the boy and girl next door. That the image had only coincidental resemblance to the people they actually were was irrelevant; happy-go-lucky was what the public was buying during the war, so that's the way June and Van were sold. But June kept at it, working in TV, dinner theater, whatever the market offered. She always made a living.

I knew June well; in fact, we used the house she had lived in with her husband Dick Powell as the house Stefanie Powers and I lived in in *Hart to Hart*. June was fun and, to be honest, rather flirtatious.

Because Dick was widely liked and respected, nobody seemed interested in seeing if there was any actual intent behind June's flirtatiousness, but lightning struck when she made *The McConnell Story* with Alan Ladd. Nobody really knows what goes on in anybody else's marriage, but June must have had some degree of discontent, and Alan had been unhappy with his wife, Sue Carol, for years.

Sue had been an actress at the tail end of the silent days, a cute little thing with some of Clara Bow's irrepressible spirit. But she didn't like talkies—or talkies didn't like her—so in 1939 she became an agent. She had a client list that included Peter Lawford, Rory Calhoun, and Sheila Ryan.

Alan had been happily married to his first wife when Sue heard him on the radio one day. She fell in love with his voice before she fell in love with him. She called the radio station and set up a meeting, and that was that. Alan was gorgeous: blond hair, green eyes, a tight swimmer's body. Sue was a goner.

I don't know that Alan had the same deep feelings for Sue that she had for him, but he went along with her infatuation, probably because he thought she might be able to get him into the movie business in a big way. He divorced his wife and, in 1942, married Sue—and became her fourth husband. That same year, she got him the lead in *This Gun for Hire*, a film I later remade for television.

That movie fired the starting gun for Alan's starring career, which culminated in 1952 and *Shane*, in which he gives a lovely performance. That movie was something of an accident—Paramount had given him bad scripts for years before that, so he had already decided to leave the studio when he made *Shane*. He went over to Warners for 10 percent of the gross on all the pictures he made for them, as well as ownership of the negative—probably the richest deal in the business at the time. Later, Natalie made a movie for Alan's company, a little B called *A Cry in the Night*, with Edmond O'Brien.

Alan was at Warner Bros. when he met June Allyson. Their affair became an open secret. Somebody who worked on the picture told me that Sue Carol would barge onto the stage where her husband was filming, bang on Alan's dressing room door, and yell, "Alan, come on out. I know you're in there!"

He fell in love with June, but neither of them was willing to divorce. Alan was already drinking at that point, and the wear and tear was beginning to show in his face. June went back to Dick Powell until Dick died in 1963, while Alan stayed with Sue. And then his drinking really picked up.

I got to know Sue and Alan before he made *The McConnell Story*, when I dated Carol Lee, Sue's daughter from a previous marriage. They both approved of me as a potential match, and Sue, a little round-faced woman, six years older than Alan, couldn't have been nicer, while I couldn't have been happier with Carol Lee.

Alan died from an overdose of pills in 1964, and it was generally felt that he committed suicide, even though his death was officially ruled accidental. (There had been another incident about eighteen months earlier, when Alan had been wounded by a self-inflicted gunshot.)

He had been terribly self-conscious about almost everything—his talent, his height, the decline in his career. In fact, at five foot six, he wasn't all that short. There were plenty of actors who were shorter—Chaplin and Cagney, among others—but it didn't bother them the way it bothered Alan. And I think he might also have been consumed by a terrible guilt over how he treated his first wife, whom I gathered he loved very much.

When I knew them, Alan and Sue seemed content, if not blissful. Whatever was plaguing her husband, Sue was unable to remedy it. She never remarried.

As for June, after Dick died, she remarried and kept as busy as she could. In retrospect, I think she was a far more interesting woman than her screen image, or the times, ever allowed her to show. The times were changing, and the girl next door was moving away from the movies and into television. But, for a time, June was America's ideal young woman.

INTERMISSION I

I'd like to pause in this procession of leading ladies to pay a belated but sincere tribute to character actresses. When I was growing up, I was always pleased to see Eve Arden's name in the cast, because I knew she'd come in and expertly deliver cynical one-liners that would puncture the pretensions of the other characters, if not the entire movie.

Eve Arden's characters were always lamenting their inability to attract a man. Actually, Eve was quite attractive, although her husband, the actor Brooks West, was an alcoholic who didn't work much. They stayed married for more than forty years, although Eve had several long-running affairs. I knew Eve and found her to be a very warm and open person.

She was probably the best at what she did, but there were others, as well. Before Eve, there were wonderful actresses like Edna May Oliver and Marie Dressler. Their job was to speak for the audience, and deliver some pointed humor at the expense of the other characters and, often, themselves.

Take Thelma Ritter, for instance. She got off some of Joseph L. Mankiewicz's best one-liners in *All About Eve* ("Everything but the bloodhounds snappin' at her rear end"), and backed up Jimmy Stewart in *Rear Window*. Thelma didn't hide her light under a bushel; she got nominated for six Academy Awards.

Thelma was pretty much what she was typically cast as: a working-class woman from Brooklyn. This may well be one of the reasons she played her parts so well. She had been on the stage, but never in a hit, and became much more successful in the movies. Before her film career took off, her husband made his living by being a contestant on radio and TV game shows. I was lucky enough to work with her in one of my first movies, *With a Song in My Heart*. I was too green to ask her a lot of questions about style and technique, but I was sufficiently aware to notice that she was a nervous actress—nervous about getting it right.

A few years later, she was part of the cast of *Titanic*, with Barbara Stanwyck and me. She was friends with Barbara, and was aware of the relationship that developed between us. Unlike her characters, who tended to blurt out whatever was on their mind, Thelma was very discreet by nature, and never spoke to anyone about the affair. Although Thelma was most often used as a comedienne, she was a terrific dramatic actress; I defy anyone to watch her performances in *Pickup on South Street* or *Birdman of Alcatraz* and not be simultaneously moved and impressed.

Character actresses like Thelma often shone with a brighter light than the supposed stars of the movies. In a sense, that was their job; their screen time was limited, and their dialogue often more pointed than what was written for the leads. They were like pinch hitters in baseball, paid to advance the offense, i.e., the plot or characters.

I knew Maureen Stapleton before she worked with Natalie, Larry Olivier, and me in *Cat on a Hot Tin Roof*. She was a thoroughly lovable woman, a devoted fan of old movies. I once gave her autographs of Clark Gable and Carole Lombard that I'd gotten at the golf course at the Bel-Air Country Club. Maureen couldn't have been any more thrilled if I'd given her a piece of the True Cross.

Maureen was nervous. About everything. She absolutely refused to fly, so came to England to play Big Mama via ocean liner. We were already rehearsing in Liverpool when Maureen arrived a few days late, and I'm sure she had walked up the stairs because she was frightened to take the elevator.

Besides being a superb actress and timid about traveling, Maureen was one of the legendary show-business alcoholics, although it didn't seem to lessen the affection that people had for her. What was amazing was that it never interfered with her work. She drank at night and on

Thelma Ritter

the weekends, and was Johnny-on-the-spot in the morning. Neil Simon even wrote a semibiographical play about Maureen, called *The Ginger-bread Lady*, that starred . . . Maureen.

Drunk or sober, Maureen was totally uninhibited. She regaled Larry Olivier and me with a story about a hot and heavy affair she was having with George Abbott—how he was ninety years old but couldn't keep his hands off her. She paid great and specific tribute to his remarkable standards of sexual performance and staying power. Larry and I would just nod our heads in amazement . . . and envy.

One night after rehearsal, Larry, Maureen, Natalie, and I went out for a night of drinking. (Larry liked to drink, but never when he was working.) The rest of us got slightly tipsy, but Maureen was totally soused, literally falling-down drunk. Larry and I had to carry her to bed, and just as we got her comfortable, her bladder let loose, and she wet the bed.

Well, we hadn't bargained on that, but Larry didn't take it personally. He took her toes and began the old nursery rhyme in a singsong voice: "This little piggy went to market, this little piggy stayed home . . ." He ended up by saying, "And this little piggy went wee-wee-wee-wee all over the bed!"

As an actress, Maureen always became the character, became what she had to play. That might have been one of the reasons she drank to such excess—she kept losing herself. A dear woman; everybody who knew Maureen adored her. Especially me.

Another of my favorite people was Ann Rutherford. Ann had a strong career in the 1930s and 1940s playing Polly Benedict opposite Mickey Rooney in the Andy Hardy films, and she's one of Vivien Leigh's sisters in *Gone with the Wind*, which ought to be sufficient grounds for immortality for any actress.

Ann never really made the transition to the name above the title. Her last big picture was *Adventures of Don Juan* opposite Errol Flynn. It was always hard to get any attention if you were making a movie with

Maureen Stapleton

Flynn, who was much more gorgeous than any of his leading ladies, with the possible exception of Olivia de Havilland.

But Ann didn't mind one bit. She knew that the movie business was brutal and was happy just to have survived. As a matter of fact, Ann may have been the most positive person I've ever met. She believed in belief.

Ann was the daughter of a man who once sang at the Metropolitan Opera. She broke into the movies at a low-budget outfit called Mascot when she was only seventeen. She appeared in serials, and she worked opposite Gene Autry, which meant that Gene's horse got more footage than she did. For a girl who began her career at Mascot, MGM was a plush country club, and Ann enjoyed every minute of it.

Ann's first husband was Dave May, the heir to the May Company. That marriage didn't last, but her second, to William Dozier, was successful. Dozier was one of those movie industry guys who was more interesting for whom he married than for what he achieved. Dozier had previously been married to Joan Fontaine, and today he's best known for producing the *Batman* TV series. (My future wife, Jill St. John, was in the pilot!)

Ann always had her eyes open. She told me that one of the most important moments of her life occurred during the filming of an unimportant picture called *Waterfront Lady*. She looked up one day and noticed an actor named Jack LaRue playing a small part as a bartender. Only a few years earlier, LaRue had been an up-and-coming star at Paramount as a sort of George Raft in training.

Ann asked what Jack was doing in such a throwaway part, and they told her that he hadn't saved his money when he was starring. Now he was broke and took whatever he could get.

That was it—a light dawned. Ann was a naturally sensible woman, and she became determined to never find herself in Jack LaRue's shoes. Although she was at MGM, earning MGM money for years—she started at three hundred dollars a week—she took the bus to work. She told me she saved for three years before she went so far as to buy a car. She was glad she did, too, because every six months she would notice how all the contract players would be sweating over whether or not the studio would pick up their options for another six months of employment. Ann saw stark fear on the faces of the girls who'd spent their money on dresses and furs and were suddenly out of work with no savings.

That's when the casting couch could come into play, as a sort of insurance policy for starlets who thought they were on the bubble between getting dropped and maintaining their jobs.

But Ann was like Scarlett O'Hara—she was never going to be hungry.

While Louis B. Mayer adored Ann because she incarnated thrift, one of his cherished virtues, he did try to take advantage of what he thought were her fears of impoverishment. When her option time would come up, he would call her into his office and tell her the studio wanted to keep her, they had big plans for her and so forth, but they couldn't afford to give her the raise her contract mandated.

Now, both of them knew this was pure fantasy; MGM was the only studio in Hollywood that never lost money during the Depression, and the Andy Hardy pictures routinely grossed ten times their cost. Besides the Hardy pictures, Ann was also working regularly in a popular series of films with Red Skelton.

But Mayer played his sad song for all it was worth, and in response Ann would wave her little bankbook and show Mayer how much money she'd saved out of her salary. Mayer would graciously capitulate and give her the raise. It was a game they both enjoyed playing for years.

When MGM loaned out Clark Gable to David Selznick and leveraged that into the distribution rights for *Gone with the Wind*, they threw Ann into the cast as well to play Scarlett's sister Carreen. It was a minor role, and Ann didn't really have much to do. She told me that she had already been playing leading parts, and in the back of her mind she thought this one was a comedown. And she would conclude that anecdote by saying "And that, my dear, is why actors have no business deciding what to play or what not to play."

MGM was known in the trade as the Tiffany studio, but even Ann

Ann Rutherford

was astonished at the extent to which David Selznick lavished time and money on his pet project. She told me that her costumes had layers and layers of petticoats beneath the dresses. She went to Selznick and said he could save a lot of money by not bothering with such elaborate costuming. The audience would never know the difference.

"But *you'll* know," he replied, arguing that the wardrobe would help her with the part—that she would be able to play a rich landowner's daughter with more credibility if her costumes lived up to the standard of living of the O'Haras. What I thought, when she told me the story, was that Selznick's rationalization might very well hold true for Vivien Leigh, who was in practically every scene of the movie, but that it might not be relevant for Ann, who was in about eight scenes. But it was David Selznick's movie, and he did almost everything right in making it.

Ann loved her years at MGM and was always grateful that she hadn't ended up working for Jack Warner, who thought nothing of purposely casting actors in bad pictures in order to exact revenge for real or imagined slights. Of course, this would also depress their value on the open market when they finally left the studio. Warners did that to Kay Francis, and Bette Davis always thought they did it to her as well. "Jack Warner was always selling people down the river," Ann would complain.

Ann finally left MGM around the end of World War II and by 1950 had retired to Beverly Hills. She got out while the getting was good. By then, MGM and the rest of the studios were in free fall and shrinking their contract lists. It would have killed Ann to see the studio she loved deteriorate at such a rapid pace.

As it was, she returned there in 1972 for a few days' work in a James Garner picture called *They Only Kill Their Masters*, and she was appalled. The studio that had been making eighteen pictures simultaneously in 1939 was now down to making only one. All the departments were closed; there was no makeup department, there was no camera department, there were no actors or writers or directors under contract. It was a shell operation.

For the rest of her long life—she died in 2012—she was a delight, a positive person who was never a Pollyanna, but who just felt lucky to have been a part of the greatest studio at the most prosperous and creative time of its corporate life.

MGM gave her more than a livelihood; it taught her to appreciate fine things. For instance, the studio prop department often outfitted sets with authentic antiques they'd buy in Europe and ship over to Culver City. On top of the tables they placed porcelain statues, and that triggered a fascination that led to Ann collecting antique porcelain for the rest of her life. In less abstract matters, Ann would talk about making *Pride and Prejudice* with Larry Olivier, and how she developed a huge crush on him that was unfortunately unrequited.

By the time Ann died, MGM had ceased to exist as a functioning movie studio. It was a brutal demonstration of the fact that nothing lasts forever.

But you know what does last? The movies the great studios made. The films that MGM churned out are still around, and still riveting audiences.

That, at least, is something. Maybe everything.

THE FIFTIES

When I arrived at 20th Century Fox in 1949, the first thing I did was crawl all over the lot. I was fascinated by how everything was done—how the various shots were edited into what seemed to be a seamless whole; how old costumes from the wardrobe department were revamped to look brand new; how the lighting made rickety flats look like real rooms.

Like every movie studio, Fox was just awash in physically beautiful women. You would encounter gorgeous every ten feet. It was not an environment for an ascetic personality. I was nineteen when I began there, so it goes without saying that I had great times on and off the lot. No apologies, no regrets.

One of my publicity dates was with a young Rita Moreno. I say "publicity date" because it was set up by the studio publicity department, and, while Rita was stunning, she was also very involved with Marlon Brando at that time and for a long time afterward. I liked Rita, but I liked Marlon, too, and wasn't about to poach on his territory. She knew it, and I knew it, but we went out a couple of times, closely accompanied by photographers. It was the way the game was played, because the studio set the rules.

I started out in shallow water—I made tests. I tested opposite almost every actress that Fox was thinking of signing. I tested opposite superb actresses, I tested opposite women who were the mistresses of powerful executives at the studio, I tested opposite women who should have used quotation marks when they listed their occupation as actress.

And I tested opposite Marilyn Monroe.

Marilyn. Everyone always wants to know about Marilyn.

I have no horror stories to tell. I thought she was a terrific woman and I liked her very much. When I knew her, she was a warm, fun girl. She was obviously nervous about the test we did together, but so was I. In any case, her nervousness didn't disable her in any way; she performed in a thoroughly professional manner. She behaved the same way in *Let's Make It Legal*, the film we later made—nervous, but eager and up to the task.

Obviously, she was extremely attractive, and she already had that special quality of luscious softness about her. She was completely nonthreatening, unless you were another woman trying to hold onto your man.

Everyone knew that she was the girlfriend of Johnny Hyde, a powerful agent at William Morris. Whenever I saw them together, Johnny gave every indication of being attentive and loving, so I'm inclined to believe that the relationship was a very positive thing for Marilyn. For Johnny, maybe not. For one thing, he was married; for another, he died young, of a heart attack in 1950.

Certainly, it was positive professionally; Johnny got Marilyn the part in John Huston's *The Asphalt Jungle* that made everybody sit up and take notice. Given Johnny's presence in her life, I made sure that my attraction to Marilyn came across as nothing more than professional admiration.

After we made *Let's Make It Legal*, Marilyn went her way, and I went mine. She became the biggest star on the Fox lot, and, along with Elizabeth Taylor, the biggest female star on the planet.

Years later, Marilyn began dropping by the house where Natalie and I lived. Our connection was through Pat Newcomb, her publicist. I had known Pat since our childhood. She had also worked for me and often accompanied Marilyn to our house. I bought a car from Marilyn—a black Cadillac with black leather interior.

Marilyn was relaxed and enjoyed herself with us, except for one time when Conroy, a black Lab that Bing Crosby gave me, growled at her. To this day I don't know what happened. Conroy was a happy dog, but there was something about Marilyn he didn't like. They say dogs know when an earthquake is coming. Maybe Conroy sensed something profoundly off-center about her.

I never saw the Marilyn of the nightmare anecdotes—the terribly insecure woman who needed pills and champagne to anesthetize her from life, and who reached a place where she couldn't get out more than a couple of consecutive sentences in front of a camera.

When I would talk with other actors, such as Tony Curtis, about their experience of acting with Marilyn, they described it as being like working with a small child or an animal. If the animal manages to do its part right, that's the take they're going to use, whether you are any good or not, which is why actors hate to work with them. In *Some Like It Hot*, Tony and Jack Lemmon had to nail every take, because Billy Wilder had no choice but to use the takes in which Marilyn was good, or even adequate—there was no guarantee she would be able to do a scene more than once.

Clearly, Marilyn had tremendous problems, and they got worse as she got older. She was prone to depression and was terribly anxious about her level of competence—another actress who was frightened of her own profession. The result was that she projected her insecurity onto everyone who was working with her. Her co-workers lived their lives in a state of terrible nervous tension—Was she going to show up? And if she did, would she be able to get anything done?

The audience doesn't care about that kind of thing—all they have to go by are the finished films, and Marilyn was generally excellent in them. But the people who made the movies were all too aware of how difficult it had been to get the movies made, and how much over budget they went because of her. At times, when you talked to people in the industry about Marilyn, you'd sense the same sort of hostility that the guys at Paramount expressed on the subject of Betty Hutton.

One thing about Marilyn: She *needed* to be a star, not out of garden-variety professional ambition, but as a means of validating herself, of proving that her father had made a terrible mistake when he abandoned her mother and her. Making it was the only way she had of proving that everybody who had refused to take her seriously, who had taken advantage of her when she was a young actress around town, was wrong. Yet the bigger she got, the more her insecurities increased. The more her insecurities increased, the harder it became for her to deal with the stardom she wanted so badly. A vicious circle.

Marilyn had an innately luminous quality that she was quite conscious of—she could turn it on or off at will. The problem was that she didn't really believe that it was enough. My second wife, Marion, knew her quite well; she and Marilyn had modeled together for several years, and were signed by Fox at the same time, where they were known as "The Two M's." Marion told stories about how the leading cover girls of that time would show up to audition for modeling jobs. If Marilyn came in to audition, they would all look at each other and shrug. Marilyn was going to get the job, and they all knew it. She had that much connection to the camera.

I got the feeling that because Marilyn hadn't had any family to speak of when she was growing up, she always gravitated toward empathy or strength, or supposed strength, which was the basis for most of her relationships. Pat Newcomb was completely dedicated to her; it was a bond that was more familial than professional.

Men with whom she became romantically involved—Elia Kazan, Arthur Miller, Frank Sinatra, even Joe DiMaggio—were all assertive by nature and seemed to have all the answers; people on whom she became emotionally dependent, such as Paula and Lee Strasberg, were even more so. I don't think there's any question that Marilyn was deeply disturbed at the end of her life. Part of the reason they pay you in show business is to be there on time, and Marilyn could no longer do that. Schedules and budgets were kindling for her wavering temperament.

When Marilyn died, Pat Newcomb was utterly devastated; Marilyn had been like a sister to her, a very close sister, and she took her death as a personal failure. Marilyn's death has to be considered one of show business's great tragedies. That sweet, nervous girl I knew when we were both starting out became a legend who has transcended the passing of time, transcended her own premature death.

I wonder if her immortality would give her any sense of satisfaction. Somehow I doubt it.

Marilyn's story is evenly split between her years of stardom, when the whole world knew who she was and cared passionately, and the years before, when nobody was aware of her and nobody cared. Just before Marilyn met Johnny Hyde and her life changed for the better, just before we tested and made a movie together, Marilyn was living at the Hollywood Studio Club, one of the more fascinating places in Hollywood history.

It was nothing more or less than a chaperoned dormitory for young girls, and was in operation from 1916 to 1975.

The Studio Club came about in this way: Before World War I, the movies hit in a big way, and thousands of young people of both sexes began flooding Hollywood each and every year. If they had saved some money, they could get cheap space at one of the dozens of garden court apartment complexes that dotted southern California.

And if they didn't have any money, they could double up, or triple up. And if they *really* didn't have any money, girls could stay at the Studio Club, which was built by private subscription. In the early days, actresses such as Mae Busch, ZaSu Pitts, and Janet Gaynor were all boarders. Actually, a lot of its residents became more famous as wives than as actresses. Dorris Bowdon, who played Rosasharn in *The Grapes of Wrath*, later married Nunnally Johnson, who wrote the script for the film, and had a long and happy life with that excellent writer.

The idea for the club began when a group of ambitious young women began having meetings at the Hollywood Public Library to read plays and discuss strategies for getting into the movies. One of the librarians began to get concerned about the safety of girls who had to live in cheap hotels, and began soliciting funds to rent an old house for them on Carlos Avenue. Constance DeMille, the wife of Cecil B., was crucial in the financial foundation of the club, as was Mary Pickford.

In the early 1920s, many of the studios and a lot of businessmen donated money for the construction of a permanent building specifically to house the Studio Club. Their generosity was stimulated partly by altruism, but also by alarm. The three huge scandals of the early 1920s—Fatty Arbuckle's manslaughter trial, the William Desmond Taylor murder, and Wallace Reid's death from the effects of drug addiction—scared the entire industry. In order to forestall censorship, they needed to emphasize propriety whenever possible, and the Studio Club was a perfect vehicle to embody the God-fearing nature of Hollywood. Famous Players-Lasky—the forerunner of Paramount—donated $10,000, and MGM and Universal $5,000 each. Norma Talmadge kicked in $5,000.

The project cost $250,000 and opened in 1926 at 1215 Lodi Place, just south of Sunset Boulevard, in the heart of Hollywood. It was a three-story Mediterranean building designed by Julia Morgan, who designed San Simeon for William Randolph Hearst. Each room at the club had a nameplate identifying the people who had contributed at least a thousand dollars to the building fund. There were rooms named for Douglas Fairbanks, Howard Hughes, Gloria Swanson, and Harold Lloyd, among others.

The club could house eighty women, who initially paid ten dollars a week for a room shared with two others, or fifteen dollars a week for a room with one other woman. There were modest age requirements; you couldn't be younger than eighteen or older than thirty. One of the few times they waived the age requirements was for Linda Darnell, who was only sixteen when she arrived. The club offered classes and also offered plays and fashion shows. The longest a girl could stay was three years. It wasn't a bad place to live at all; the girls had a way of bonding with each other, and the club made no effort to impart a religious message to the residents. Alcohol was a no-no, but smoking was permitted. It goes without saying that men were not allowed in the

Marjorie Williams (center), director of the Hollywood Studio Club,
stands with the girls at Carlos Avenue clubhouse

rooms; when a girl had a date, the guy would wait downstairs until the girl came down a luxurious staircase that led from the lobby to the dorm rooms. By the 1930s, the building's yearly budget ran to around $50,000, and most of that was covered by the girls' rents; any deficit was made up by the national YWCA.

Marilyn lived there for a little more than a year, from 1948 to 1949, in rooms 307 and 334. She told me her rent was fifty dollars a month, which included two meals a day—a great deal for a girl struggling to make ends meet. She liked to reminisce that the reason she posed for the famous nude photographs was to get enough money to pay her rent at the club. (People at the club, however, would insist that she had left there by the time of that photo session.)

The girls who resided at the club could tell who among them was likely to make it. There was a certain inner resolution, a confidence, possessed by those who were heading for bigger things. I was told that when Marilyn lived there she was quiet—I believe it—and was usually carrying a book. When she came down for breakfast, the other girls would notice and be impressed, but not jealous. There was always something vulnerable and likeable about her.

During the Depression, when I was just starting to watch movies, jobs were scarce, and times were tough. If you were an average girl trying to break into the movies, and were unable to get space at the Studio Club, you might be rooming with five or six other girls in a bungalow apartment. Two girls would share a bed, one would take the couch, one would be on a reclining chair, and whoever drew the short straw would be on the floor with a pillow. The girl who had worked most recently would pay for groceries, and someone was designated to stay close to home to answer the phone, just in case a job came through for any of the housemates. None of the girls had a car—you either took the streetcar, or counted on your boyfriend, if you had one, to take you where you needed to go. Even under these conditions, you could count on a couple of the girls not being able to make their share of the rent.

Diana Serra Cary is a fine writer who did time as a child star in silent movies as Baby Peggy. She wrote about the bizarre circumstances of Hollywood in those years: "There were two Hollywoods, the packaged export on which our very lives depended and the real thing, on which most of us practically starved to death . . . Among a dozen of our close friends, not one family could stay on top of the electric, gas, water and telephone bills as well. One or the other was always being shut off or 'temporarily disconnected.' This brought into existence an unspoken code of conduct that helped us cope with an abnormal situation which, for the time being at least, was our way of life.

"If we were the ones whose telephone was working (but whose water had been turned off) . . . we let the next-door neighbor, who was without phone service, call . . . and she in turn gave us enough water to make supper. If our gas was off it was no disgrace to put the makings of dinner in a roaster and march upstairs to Mrs. Lundquist's kitchen. There we cooked the meal while Mrs. Lundquist was downstairs using our phone. The combinations and reciprocations were endless, and fortunately everyone possessed a sense of the ridiculous, which made it possible to laugh instead of cry over the way things were."

By these standards, which were more or less normal for all those who didn't have a contract at a major studio during the 1930s, the Hollywood Studio Club was nirvana. The club would even carry you until you could make good on your back rent.

There's a semifamous movie called *Stage Door* that owed a great deal to the Studio Club. The basis for the 1937 movie was a play by George S. Kaufman and Edna Ferber about a theatrical boardinghouse in New York called the Footlights Club, a women-only establishment like the Studio Club. Kaufman and Ferber were high-end writers, and the movie's cast included Katharine Hepburn, Ginger Rogers, and Lucille Ball, but Gregory La Cava, the director, thought the script needed some salt and pepper.

La Cava sent his mistress, an actress named Doris Nolan, over to the Studio Club to hang out and listen to the women talk. "Find me some dialogue that's alive," he instructed her. "Get some case histories. Who are these kids? Why do they want to be in pictures? Where do they come from? What was their home like? Small town? Why did they leave home to come here? Are they having any success? Have they been to the casting couch? Was it worth it? *I want it in their own language.*"

Stage Door was a big hit, and its success inspired Warner Bros. to announce production of a movie starring Olivia de Havilland and Anita Louise that would actually be set at the Hollywood Studio Club. Unfortunately, the movie never happened.

Others who lived there at one time or another included Barbara Hale, Donna Reed, Frances Bergen (wife of Edgar, mother of Candice), Kim Novak, Maureen O'Sullivan, Sharon Tate, Dorothy Malone, Gale Storm, Marie Windsor, Linda Darnell, Rita Moreno, Barbara Eden, Evelyn Keyes, Sally Struthers, and Ayn Rand. (Most of the inhabitants were aspiring actresses, but not all; if you wanted to work in the movies, as a writer or editor or designer or even as a secretary, you could get into the club.)

All the girls had money problems, or they wouldn't have lived there, but evidently Ayn Rand was unusually broke even by the standards of the club. One philanthropist gave fifty dollars to be earmarked for the poorest of the girls. The director of the club chose Rand, who thanked the club for the money and promptly used it to buy black lingerie. Rand, of course, wanted to be a writer, and she had gotten a role in Cecil B. DeMille's *King of Kings* as an extra. It was on that film that she met the man she would marry, and the story goes that she wrote *Night of January 16th* while living at the Studio Club.

Evelyn Keyes was a young woman who had been raised in Georgia and had an accent to match. That accent would eventually work to her advantage when she was cast as one of Scarlett O'Hara's sisters in *Gone with the Wind*. Several years before that, her marriage had broken up, and she went to the Studio Club because she had no place else to stay.

She thought she had died and gone to heaven. She appreciated the club because it was respectable—it was one of the few spots in Hollywood she thought her mother would approve of. "It was a place where you were protected and it was reasonable," she said. "They weren't trying to make money. They were trying to make a haven for young girls."

Marie Windsor told me that it was a great place to live because all the boarders there were at the same stage of their lives—the beginning, before they'd had many disappointments or failures, and the world was still opening up before them. Marie said that Marilyn Monroe moved out the same week she moved in. She didn't know her then, but got to know her a little later, about the time Marilyn was making *The Asphalt Jungle*. She liked her, but she said that one of the executives had to tell Marilyn to come to work in clean clothes. (I guess MGM had higher standards than the Studio Club.)

Marie got a job as a cigarette girl at the Mocambo from a want ad that went up on the bulletin board at the club. The Mocambo was where she met the producer Arthur Hornblow, who liked her and got her work with the choreographer Leroy Prinz. After that, Marie was off to the races, and a nice career that included working for Stanley Kubrick on *The Killing*. That was the way careers began in the Hollywood of that time. Coincidence, luck, timing, eagerness—pretty much the same way careers have always begun.

Kim Novak was remembered as being very neat and clean—nobody could look more glamorous in a man's white shirt and Levi's. Kim never liked Hollywood, or, for that matter, the movies; she didn't want to leave the cozy confines of the club, which had by then raised the maximum length of stay to five years. After she left, she donated money and clothes to the club.

I know that my friend Jeffrey Hunter courted Barbara Rush when she was living at the club; in fact, the club gave a party when they were engaged. And there were various legends that may or may not have been true. I once heard a story that a hotel clerk registered at the Biltmore as a cousin of King Alfonso of Spain. Hollywood has always been impressed by titles, but she couldn't pay her bill. Somehow or another, the wife of the actor Antonio Moreno took her in and placed her at the Studio Club, where nobody was aware of her fraud.

When I was a young man around Hollywood, stories about life at the club were legion, though almost all of them would be rated PG-13 at worst. For the most part, its reputation was quite good, but there was the occasional embarrassment; one of the girls was murdered in front of the club by her boyfriend, who then proceeded to kill himself. Evelyn Keyes remembered that pregnancies were not exactly uncommon among the residents. During its final decade, the club was home to people like Sharon Tate, Nancy Kwan, Susan Saint James, and Sally Struthers.

Eventually it was overtaken by changing times. The idea of a chaperoned dormitory became gradually passé; many girls opted for the simpler alternative of shacking up with their boyfriends. The charter of the club expanded the eligibility requirements to include dancers and models, but it began losing lots of money; in 1971 it stopped serving meals and began to function as a regular hotel in addition to taking care of the girls.

The Studio Club finally closed in 1975, and the building was awarded landmark status in 1979. Today it is still the property of the Los Angeles YWCA.

In the fifty-nine-year history of the building on Lodi Place, some ten thousand women lived there.

Ayn Rand always retained a soft spot for the club, and wrote about it: "The Studio Club is the only organization I know of personally that carries on, quietly and modestly, this great work which is needed so badly—help for young talent. It not only provides human, decent living accommodations which a poor beginner could not afford anywhere else, but it provides that other great necessity of life: understanding. It makes a beginner feel that he is not, after all, an intruder, with all the world laughing at him and rejecting him at every step, but that there are people who consider it worthwhile to dedicate their work to helping and encouraging him."

Notice Rand's use of the masculine pronoun. Interesting. As was the Studio Club, a place that could only have existed as part of the movie business, and only in Hollywood.

* * *

People sometimes ask me if I can identify any defining characteristic common to the women I've worked with over a nearly seventy-year career. The truth is that the vast majority of those who came up during the studio system were well defined in their own minds. They knew what they wanted, and if they didn't, they didn't last long. Almost all of them had endured hardships as kids, and as show business invariably presented its own kinds of hardships, they were by nature and necessity survivors.

All of them were aware that they had a limited period of opportunity within which to achieve and consolidate stardom; most of them were likewise aware that stardom is a finite state and that eventually that state would pass. At that point, the pressure would be off, so for most of them working could be more of a pleasure at sixty or seventy than it had been at thirty. I also picked up a certain sense of guilt—a number of them felt that they had shortchanged their families and their children in the pursuit of professional success.

Hearing that made me respect people like Claudette Colbert and Kate Hepburn all the more, because they had the self-awareness to forgo having children. That may be a partial reason why they had the successful careers they did—their eyes were fixed firmly on the prize, and they weren't hampered by competing emotional or psychological demands.

Most of these women centered their lives around their acting, but not everybody shared that consuming passion. Doris Day worked hard for a lot of years, and moreover she was a triple threat—she could sing, she was a successful comedienne, and she was excellent in serious roles. But it gradually got to the point where she didn't want to be in the business anymore, and she walked away when she was only fifty or so, something very few performers do. The ones who leave, who have the fortitude and the lack of ego to do something else with their lives, are particularly interesting to me.

Doris was a band singer during World War II and got into musicals at Warner Bros., where she made a big splash because of her sunny smile and creamy singing voice.

She projected midwestern pluck and optimism, and a kind of scrubbed quality in spite of a private life that didn't always conform to her public image. She didn't get a lot of love from the critics, who treated her as an offshoot of June Allyson, and who tend to disparage anyone who has enormous commercial success.

Let me tell you something: Doris could do *anything* asked of her, do it well, and make it look easy. She could do light comedy with Cary Grant; she could do drama with Jim Cagney; she could do thrillers for Hitchcock.

She certainly had need of inner reserves of optimism because her husband, Marty Melcher, was a crook and left her nearly broke, then conveniently died, leaving Doris holding an empty bag.

Doris did what one of her screen characters would have done: she rolled up her sleeves and got to work replenishing her bank account. And when the job was done, she decided to do what would make her happier than show business: working with animals and enjoying her life. She declined every movie offer, even the good ones, and she even resisted appearances on the Academy Awards—she just wasn't interested in keeping her hand in anymore.

It's not a viewpoint I share—I have a passion for show business, always have and always will—but it's a viewpoint I respect. Doris was a performer who endured for a very long time. She always gave great value for the money; she earned my respect and that of the audience.

Susan Hayward was a Brooklyn girl, the daughter of a transit worker. She was also a movie star. She worked hard, she treated people well, and she had a great reputation around the Fox lot. Among the people she treated kindly was one Robert Wagner.

The name of the movie we appeared in together was *With a Song in My Heart*, in which Susan played Jane Froman, a popular singer who made a comeback after almost getting killed in a plane crash. I played a young soldier existing in a catatonic state who was lured back to life by Jane Froman's singing to me.

It sounds corny. It *was* corny, but it also happened to be a true story, and Susan played it for all it was worth, as did I. Shooting that short scene took about three days, and Susan was so deeply into the emotions of the moment that she was brought to tears over and over again. She worked very hard to give me everything I needed to play the scene, and her sincerity and passion compensated for my inexperience.

The picture was directed by Walter Lang, who became a good friend, and edited by Watson Webb, ditto. It was a phenomenal break for a young actor, and suddenly, I had a career. Susan got an Oscar nomination for the film, one of five she would earn.

By the time we worked together, Susan was a name-above-the-title star, with a rapidly growing list of hit pictures, but she never had it easy. She'd tested for the part of Scarlett O'Hara in 1939, but it was too soon for her; she didn't have Vivien Leigh's rapturous beauty or, at that point, her skill set.

Susan was one of those stars who put the pieces together slowly, film by film, year by year. Her first big picture was DeMille's *Reap the Wild Wind*, with John Wayne and Paulette Goddard. She worked again with the Duke in *The Fighting Seabees*, back at his home base of Republic, which only indicates Paramount's lack of faith in her—they would never have lent out anybody they valued to Republic.

She worked steadily throughout the 1940s, and for a time she was at Walter Wanger's operation, which undoubtedly meant that she was either being chased around Wanger's desk or allowing herself to be caught. Long before Wanger shot Jennings Lang in the balls for moving in on his wife, Joan Bennett, he was well known for preying on actresses.

The 1950s were Susan's prime. She won an Oscar for *I Want to Live!*, and she was in big pictures like *The Snows of Kilimanjaro, David and Bathsheba, I'll Cry Tomorrow,* and a very good Robert Mitchum picture about rodeo cowboys called *The Lusty Men*. She made several good movies with Ty Power, and became part of his social group; Cesar Romero thought the world of her.

Susan was a physically small woman, who became close to the astrologer Carroll Righter and paid close attention to his forecasts. Her on-screen style was sexy, direct, and tough when she needed it to be. She was very much in the mold of actresses like Stanwyck and Davis, but her strong on-screen sense of self didn't carry over into her private life. Her first husband, Jess Barker, was a small-part actor who had a habit of slapping her around; they had a particularly nasty divorce involving the custody of their twin sons, and the word around the lot had it that Susan was so distraught over the situation that she attempted suicide.

Afterward, she was as big a star as ever, until her career slowed down in the 1960s. Susan stepped away for a while to concentrate on her second marriage, which was quite successful. She was set to go into television when she became ill with a brain tumor.

Susan had agreed to present the Best Actress award at the 1974 Academy Awards, but she was in failing health. My friend, the great makeup man Frank Westmore, sailed into battle and helped her out. He custom made a wig for Susan so that she could still sport her trademark red hair, and did her makeup so impeccably you never would have known she was undergoing radiation treatments. With Frank's help, Susan's last public appearance was a triumph.

She died in 1975, when she was only fifty-seven years old. Her grace, patience, and generosity with an inexperienced newcomer changed my life. I will always be in her debt.

One of the most breathtaking women I've ever seen was Jean Peters, who was at 20th Century Fox in the early and mid-1950s. I was besotted by the woman.

Jean was from Ohio—Canton, to be specific—and she was the Midwest at its best: a sincere, loving personality, to which she added stunning looks. She originally came to Hollywood as a prize for winning the Miss Ohio State pageant, and somehow or other landed the job as Tyrone Power's leading lady in *Captain from Castile* within a year of

Susan Hayward

arriving in town. She didn't have much to do in the movie, although she did it well.

Darryl Zanuck worked hard to make her a star, using her in all sorts of movies: comedies (*It Happens Every Spring*), Oscar bait (*Viva Zapata!*), and throbbing melodramas (*Niagara*).

Jean was good in everything, but she was never great. Something was lost in the space between her gorgeous face and the film running through the camera. She was beautiful on-screen, but in a slightly antiseptic way; the sensuality she had in person didn't register on celluloid, and as an actress she seemed placid, without a lot of fire.

Darryl saw the problem and attempted to elevate Jean's temperature by casting her as a tempestuous pirate queen, the sort of part that would normally be played by Maureen O'Hara, but that strategy wasn't successful, either. She worked in a couple of big hits like *Three Coins in the Fountain* and with Spencer Tracy and me in *Broken Lance*, but she ended up quitting the movie business in 1955 at the age of twenty-eight. It was all very strange; it may be that Jean was simply too inhibited for a movie career—she couldn't seem to open up in front of the camera.

But in 1957, Jean married Howard Hughes, who was never thought of as marriage material. He had had half of the women in Hollywood and could probably have had most of the other ones, as well. This was in spite of some of Hughes's personal issues. I had a brief relationship with Anita Ekberg, who had a brief relationship with Hughes, and she told me that Hughes had a problem with premature ejaculation. This meant that a lot of Hughes's relationships were probably due more to his bank account than to any of his other assets.

His marriage to Jean was hopelessly compromised as he declined into his various manias, and they spent most of their time as a couple separately. They were finally divorced, and Jean married Stan Hough, a second-generation producer who was the son of Lefty Hough, a wonderful old prop man and production manager at Fox. Stan was a good guy, and after they married Jean did some acting on TV for old times' sake.

Some of the girls around Fox were on their own, but some of them were chaperoned—very much so. Debra Paget was guarded by her mother as if she were the Crown Jewels; she wouldn't let Debra out of her sight, going so far as following her into the bathroom! This was terribly frustrating for me, because I had a major crush on Debra.

She was born in Denver, and had two sisters, who were also quite lovely, although not up to Debra's level. Eventually she went with Howard Hughes for a while (before he landed Jean Peters), a match I've always suspected took place only because Debra's mother was gob-smacked by Hughes's money.

Debra had an interesting marital history. She married her first husband in 1958, but that was annulled in a couple of months. Her next husband was the director Budd Boetticher, and they separated after only twenty-two days. Finally, she wed a Chinese-American oilman who happened to be the nephew of Madame Chiang Kai-Shek. That union lasted seven years.

Debra came to a measure of fame in the early 1950s, when she was still a teenager. She played Jimmy Stewart's doomed Indian love interest in *Broken Arrow*, and Louis Jourdan's doomed Tahitian love interest in *Bird of Paradise*. I made two movies with her: *Stars and Stripes Forever* and *White Feather*, where she again played an American Indian, although this time she managed to stay alive.

She gave Cecil B. DeMille fits on *The Ten Commandments*, because he found her inexpressive. But what he and the rest of Hollywood didn't know was that Debra was actually a dancer, not an actress. To dance with her was a beautiful and very sensual experience.

In 1960, she went to Germany to make two movies for Fritz Lang. In this country, the two films were combined into one and called *Journey to the Lost City*. Debra does a dance in the film that's reason enough to watch it—it's right up there with Rita Hayworth's "Put the Blame on Mame" number in *Gilda*.

Debra was like Rita Hayworth in that dancing released something in her that acting didn't—when she acted she was sincere and even soulful, but when she danced she was *alive*. If Darryl Zanuck had put

Debra in musicals instead of casting her as a conventional ingénue, she might have had a major career. As it was, she stopped acting in 1962, when she was only twenty-nine years old.

Most of the women I knew in that era had successful careers and somewhat compromised offscreen lives, some of which involved a great deal of pain.

For some years, I hung around with Janet Leigh and Tony Curtis. Janet was brought to the movies by Norma Shearer—small world, isn't it?—who had seen Janet's picture on her father's desk at a Sun Valley ski resort. Before you could say "seven-year contract," Janet had a deal at MGM.

When I met Janet, she had been dating Arthur Loew Jr., but he couldn't compete with Tony. Tony had energy and charm to burn, and Janet was bewitched. Janet was very much in love with Tony, but Tony . . . let's put it this way: I liked Tony a great deal. He was a guy's guy, but Tony's main object of affection was always going to be Tony. He simply had to have women adore him. Whether he was on location or at the studio, he couldn't be faithful.

Janet had not been brought up to countenance that; however much she liked the lifestyle she and Tony shared, she could not put up with infidelity indefinitely. So the marriage broke up, and Tony spent the rest of his life pollinating all the flowers he could find. Personally, I thought he was crazy to forfeit a girl with Janet's level of beauty and class, but that was Tony.

Janet was a star, but she was also a sensible woman. She took advantage of what she'd learned at MGM when she was young, and could separate the wheat from the chaff. I remember her talking about Howard Strickling, who was the director of publicity there, and his explanation of how one person could control a crowd of dozens, if not hundreds, at a promotional appearance.

"If you stay calm," Strickling told her, "the crowd stays calm. If

Janet Leigh

you act like you're going to stay there until the last autograph hunter is satisfied, they'll wait their turn." But, Strickling went on to explain, the trick is to keep moving at all times, slowly but methodically. Smile and sign, but don't stop moving toward the car. If you stop and they corner you, it's a much harder situation to handle. Janet said that Strickling's crowd psychology had always worked for her, and I might add that it's always worked for me, too.

Janet was very perceptive—and often funny—about directors. For instance, when she made *Psycho*, she realized that Hitchcock was far more interested in his shots than he was in his actors, and he would only concern himself with matters of character if an actor went off the rails. By the same token, he trusted his cast to summon whatever motivations they needed to explain the behavior that was indicated in the script. He would listen if an actor went to him for help, but he didn't have limitless reserves of patience for such guidance. His attitude was: "You are an actor. You have been hired to act. I make very few casting errors, so can we get on with our business without a lot of discussion?"

Janet realized that her character, Marion Crane, had absolutely no backstory, nothing to explain why her character was having a tawdry lunch-hour affair, so she did what Hitchcock didn't find necessary to do—she constructed an entire life for Marion before the film opens. It didn't show on-screen, but it gave Janet a feeling of conviction about her actions, which in turn convinced the audience. And, not coincidentally, made the audience that much more shocked when she was slaughtered in the shower so early in the film.

Later in life Janet had a very happy marriage to Robert Brandt, and was thrilled when the acting career of her daughter Jamie Lee took off, and she was also very proud of her daughter Kelly. Janet was a remarkably well-adjusted woman—a class act all the way.

I didn't really know what to expect when I worked with Joanne Woodward in *A Kiss Before Dying*. Joanne was a Method actress, and I came from a different school. I had consciously modeled myself after an older generation of actors, and although I had nothing against the Method, which involved summoning personal memories to authenticate emotions in a given scene, it didn't particularly work for me.

I thought then and I think now that actors should be able to rely on their imagination—one of the most important things in life. I also believe that every talent needs to use whatever is most effective for him or her. It's up to the director to find an emotional through line that makes sense of all the differing techniques and aims that the cast in a particular film embodies.

I needn't have worried about Joanne. Between scenes, she would sit and knit. While she knitted, she would think about her character and the scene she was about to shoot. She would fall into a neutral state in which her own personality receded and the character edged closer and closer to her. Gradually, finally, the character took up residence.

Joanne knew who she was, she knew how to make her process work for her in a manner that freed her up instead of locking her down. She never tried to convince anyone else that her way was *the* way. There was no stress or strain to how Joanne worked. Acting with her was a great experience.

She was born in Georgia, and she always had a trace of that soft Southern touch in her voice. Joanne was one of those huge talents like Meryl Streep—she got to the top quickly, and without any sense of strain. She was an understudy for several parts in the Broadway production of *Picnic,* which led to some TV work. She made her first movie when she was twenty-five, and her second was *A Kiss Before Dying.* You never would have known she was at such an early stage in her career; she was incredibly centered for a young actress—an old soul. After our picture, she got her Oscar for *The Three Faces of Eve,* married Paul Newman in 1958, and was off on a stellar career and, far more important, a stellar life.

I've never worked with Meryl Streep, but I know people who have, and they tell me she's a lot like Joanne—a great talent that bloomed early, and also something a little more unusual: a quality temperament that makes her a pure pleasure to work with. She's liked within the business and without, which is one reason she's had such a remarkable career; she's respected for her talent and liked for the woman she is.

Joanne married a man who was professionally like her in many ways. Paul didn't use his technique as something to set him apart, or as some sort of status symbol. He was more obviously given to dissecting the arc of a character than she was, but he was also insistent on being one of the guys.

Paul and Joanne had one of the greatest marriages I was ever privileged to witness. Not greatest show-business marriages—greatest marriages, period. Joanne's ambition extended far past her profession; she wanted to be responsible and responsive to all things. Most obviously, she had a commitment to her children. The great gift she and Paul shared was a lack of overwhelming ego; they had no pre-conceived ideas of who they were as actors. They both understood that careers are like smoke; at different times in your life, your career is going to waft in different directions, and not all of them are going to be positive. Most of it has little to do with who you are as a person or even as an actor, but that's easier to accept in concept than it is to live with when the scripts aren't arriving or the ones that are arriving are terrible. Both Paul and Joanne were completely secure within themselves. Paul never sweated if a picture or two failed; he figured that the next one might hit, and everything would be all right.

I worked with Paul and Joanne in 1969 in a good picture called *Winning*, and that was the beginning of a solid friendship. They confirmed my own sense that the best way to survive the vagaries of show business is to have a life outside of it. There is no finer example of living that principle than Paul and Joanne. They worked in the theater, they started up the Hole in the Wall Gang Camp for seriously ill kids, and Paul established the Newman's Own line of food products that has churned out hundreds of millions of dollars for charity.

Paul continued his career on a very high level until just a year or

Joanne Woodward

two before his death in 2008. I stay in touch with Joanne to this day. She remains a woman to admire and love.

Lauren Bacall became a star in her first film, *To Have and Have Not,* by channeling some of Marlene Dietrich's quality of bored hauteur. Dietrich wasn't going to pursue a man—she would simply indicate her interest, and if he was too dumb or square to do anything about it, she'd move on to the next guy.

Bacall had never acted before, so Howard Hawks had to trick out a personality for her in that first movie, and he directed her beautifully. Bacall projected brilliantly in her scenes with Bogart, so when they got married a few years later, the marriage made a lot of sense; they had an ease with each other and great on-screen timing that made you believe the marriage must have been a lot of fun.

This is emphatically not always the case with real-life married couples—Elizabeth Taylor and Richard Burton had a roaring affair that led to not one, but two unsuccessful marriages. Burton's diaries attest to their real-life sexual chemistry, but they never really struck sparks on-screen, and there were times, such as in *The Comedians,* when their love scenes were terribly phony. The same thing happened with Tom Cruise and Nicole Kidman.

Sometimes it photographs, sometimes it doesn't.

By the 1950s, leading ladies weren't just marginalized, they were endangered. To take just one obvious bellwether: Every year since 1932, the trade paper *Motion Picture Herald* had been putting out a list of the top ten box office stars. In the 1930s, women reliably held five or six of the top ten spots. By the 1940s, the average had dropped to about four, and in the 1950s, two. In 1957, no women appeared on the list at all. In the early 1960s, Elizabeth Taylor and Doris Day consistently charted,

but the fact remains that the audience and the industry as a whole became far more interested in men than women.

But then, *everything* in the film business turned upside down in the
1950s, although the events that led to the crash originated in the previous decade. The government won an antitrust suit against the movie
studios that forced them to sell off their theater chains, which the government said made them a monopoly. This meant that the studios lost
an entire profit stream.

Simultaneously, TV started draining away the audience. By the
mid-1950s, you could see the studio system was falling apart. Some of
the independents hung on—Disney, Goldwyn—but they didn't do
mass production. Rather, they were more like independent jewelers;
each of their pictures was handcrafted.

RKO went out of business after a decade of Howard Hughes's mis-
management. Darryl Zanuck opted out of running his studio; he simply
burned out. He moved to Paris and went into independent production,
making a picture a year instead of overseeing thirty, and Fox began to
have severe problems under his successor, Buddy Adler.

Unfortunately, the pictures Darryl produced in Europe (*The Roots
of Heaven, Crack in the Mirror, The Sun Also Rises*) didn't help prop Fox
up at all. Darryl made good on his losses when he produced *The Longest Day*, but there were a lot of failures before that.

Losing the theaters was a financial blow for the studios, but it was
also a psychological one. If you take the long view, it's obvious that the
movie industry has always been resistant to any form of change.
They've had to be dragged kicking and screaming into every new era.

In the nickelodeon days, they didn't want feature pictures, only shorts.
In the silent era, they didn't want sound. Then they put off color as long as
they possibly could, and then came the civil war with television. More recently, we've seen the revolution in digital production—the one change the
industry did leap into, simply because it meant a vast saving of money.

It's a mark of how psychologically conservative the movie business is that no major technological change has ever been developed in-house at a movie studio. Not one. Warners rented Western Electric's sound system; the Technicolor Corporation developed its own process and rented it out to the studios; Fox bought CinemaScope from a French inventor. And so forth. It's always the same: A tidal wave of change that begins outside the studio walls ultimately can't be resisted, and the studios finally capitulate.

And the tragic thing is that the studios could have owned all of it. They could have owned sound instead of renting it; they could have owned color instead of renting it; they could have owned NBC and CBS instead of gradually becoming subservient to them. And 20th Century Fox could have built and owned Century City instead of selling off so much prime real estate to raise money for *Cleopatra*.

Alongside the revolution that was roiling the way pictures had been made and distributed was a revolution in styles of acting and directing. Actors like Brando and James Dean worked in a different way, and there was a lot of foolish chatter about the end of "personality" acting, that the presence of Brando made actors who worked in an older style obsolete. As if you ever thought Brando was anybody but Brando.

In fact, chameleon actors like Paul Muni or Daniel Day-Lewis, performers who can create emotionally and physically unique characters from picture to picture, come along about once a generation, if that. The reasons are basic: Actors who sustain careers for a long period of time tend to have very powerful, vivid personalities. Chameleonic actors are often strangely bland when you see them on talk shows or meet them; they don't have strong personalities of their own, but they can expand at will to fill out large, well-written characters.

I would go so far as to say that acting, or at least movie acting, has always been and still is a personality business, which is proven by how many of the actors of the 1930s and 1940s survived rather nicely in the 1950s, in spite of the predictions of a lot of observers—people, I might add, who never made a movie of their own.

Still, the changes were sudden and brutal. Once MGM let Gable go, nobody was safe. The same was true of Tyrone Power at Fox, although by then Ty was anxious to get away and stretch his wings. At Fox, he worked for a straight salary; freelancing, he could get percentage deals. Ty told me he made a lot more money from a very ordinary Universal picture called *The Mississippi Gambler* than he had ever made for a movie at Fox.

Lana Turner had been a huge star in the 1940s, but sailed right through the 1950s with some huge hits like *Peyton Place* and *Imitation of Life* after being cut loose by MGM when they were going through one of their periodic convulsions.

She didn't have a particularly good reputation as an actress, but the affection I had for Lana as a person took precedence over concerns about her level of talent. In fact, I thought she was quite good in *The Bad and the Beautiful*, not to mention a movie George Cukor directed called *A Life of Her Own*, which not enough people know about.

But it's probably true that Lana needed it all working for her—a good script, and a good director to motivate her. But then, doesn't everyone? The problem was that MGM was only occasionally interested in giving their stars that kind of consistent support; their stars were expected to pull the weight of mediocre scripts and directors as a matter of course. That's why Clark Gable is primarily remembered today for two pictures: *Gone with the Wind* and *It Happened One Night*—both made away from MGM on loan-out.

Lana was one of those women who got into the movies very young—probably too young. The movies were all she really knew, and sometimes it showed in some of her naïve choices in men—seven husbands, eight if you count two marriages to Stephen Crane, not to mention affairs with Ty Power, and the late, unlamented Johnny Stompanato.

Her background was similar to Crawford's or Monroe's—an impoverished upbringing, with a missing father. Making it in the movie business was supposed to make good on all the emotional and financial deprivation of their childhoods.

Lana Turner

Supposed to.

Lana was born Julia Jean Mildred Frances Turner (her family called her Judy) in an Idaho mining town. Her father was a gambler who was beaten to death in a robbery involving his stash of money. Her mother was working in a beauty parlor, so Lana was boarded out to a family that treated her badly.

If all that wasn't grim enough, along came the Depression. Just when things couldn't get much worse, Lana and her mother moved to Hollywood, if only because they figured it was better to be warm and poor than cold and poor. Lana enrolled at Hollywood High, and one day in January 1937, she was sitting at a drugstore—it might have been Schwab's, at the corner of Sunset and Crescent Heights, on the south side, and it might have been someplace else. The legend, as spread by the columnist Sidney Skolsky, says that it was Schwab's, but you have to be careful about how much trust to put in legends.

What Lana told me is that she had cut classes at Hollywood High— she never claimed to be a scholar. Billy Wilkerson, the publisher of the *Hollywood Reporter*, spotted her, and his eyes zoomed out of his head like the wolf in a Tex Avery cartoon.

And then Billy popped the Question: "Would you like to be in the movies?" (This has always carried far more weight than the conventional question about getting married.)

Judy was young, she was quite beautiful, and she had a body that men would go to war over. Her answer was basic: "I don't know. I'd have to ask my mother."

Since the family was still in search of something that would float their lives, Mom thought it was a great idea. Billy took her to Zeppo Marx, who had quit the family comedy act to become an agent. Zeppo brought her to Warner Bros., where Mervyn LeRoy changed her name from Judy to Lana, and showcased her bouncing down the street in an unforgettable shot in *They Won't Forget* when she was all of seventeen. When Mervyn left Warners to go to MGM, he took Lana with him. She was a particularly valuable addition to the studio—with the exception of the late Jean Harlow, MGM was not really in the business of sexy, but they were about to be.

Lana went to drama school, and she was carefully placed in films where she would be noticed but wouldn't have to carry much dramatic weight—an Andy Hardy vehicle, a Dr. Kildare, some other B-level movies, then some musicals. *Ziegfeld Girl* moved her out of the promising class and into the big time. Busby Berkeley staged the musical numbers, and then there was the cast. In order of billing, they were: James Stewart, Judy Garland, Hedy Lamarr, and Lana Turner. MGM showcased her impeccably: In 1941, besides *Ziegfeld Girl,* she made *Dr. Jekyll and Mr. Hyde*—as the good girl!—*Honky Tonk* with Clark Gable, and *Johnny Eager* with Robert Taylor.

Lana's attitude toward all this was simple: Why not? As she would say, "There were girls who were prettier, more intelligent, and just as talented. Why didn't they make it? It's a question of magic. You have it or you don't, I guess."

From the beginning, Lana had that specific ability that is common to almost all great movie stars: She was open to the camera, by which I mean it didn't scare her.

By the time she made *The Postman Always Rings Twice* in 1946, she was only twenty-six, but she'd been a star for nearly ten years. I like her performance in that film. She downplays the emotion, just as the character would in real life—a woman with that kind of sexual power doesn't really have to do much more than just *be*. Look at the man and see him react. Be a trifle uninterested. Watch him grovel.

And costuming her all in white—and in shorts!—was a master stroke of design, one that contrasted strongly with John Garfield's darkness and street good looks. Throughout the 1940s Lana reigned as Hollywood's primary sex symbol. Even though she had more flops than hits in the following decade—middle age is always difficult for sex symbols—the hits were considerable.

Lana's problem was that she became known more for her life off-screen than on-screen. Specifically, her marriages began adding up.

Lana's belief system when it came to men was simple: "If you want a blueprint, here it is: lose one love, snap right back and catch another."

Her first husband was Artie Shaw, whom she wed when she was barely twenty. That lasted all of four months.

I believe that Artie took it upon himself to educate her—Artie had a terrible Henry Higgins complex, which accounts for why none of his wives (a group that included Ava Gardner) hung around long. Artie's invariable presumption was that his girl or wife of the moment was always dumber than he was, and nobody likes to be slotted into that category, even if it happens to be true.

After Artie came Stephen Crane, by whom Lana was already pregnant, only to find out that Crane's first marriage hadn't been dissolved yet. They had to get their marriage annulled in order for him to get divorced, then remarry. Quickly.

That marriage lasted a couple of years and was followed by a very public affair with Ty Power. Lana got pregnant again, and was thrilled, but Ty . . . Ty was separated from Annabella, his wife at the time, but they weren't divorced yet. It was 1947—there weren't a lot of options.

Ty told her that the choice was up to her; all he asked was that she should let him know what she decided. He left on a twelve-week airplane trip, and she got hold of him via ham radio. "I found the house today," she told him—their prearranged code for her decision to have an abortion.

When Ty returned, Lana was fully prepared to resume the affair; she figured that when he was divorced, they would marry. But Ty first avoided her, then, when they got back together, was distant. Finally, he told her the truth—he had fallen hard for Linda Christian while he was overseas. What made the situation worse was that Linda Christian had played a very minor part in Lana's film *Green Dolphin Street*.

Lana had a large emotional investment in Ty, so she took all this very hard. Ty ended up marrying Christian, who played around on him and eventually took him for a hefty divorce settlement. To the end of her life, Lana regarded Ty Power as the great love of her life, probably because he was the one who got away. I can't imagine two more beautiful people ever cohabiting on the face of the earth.

I knew Lana best in the mid-1950s. She had been at MGM since she was a teenager, so when the studio cut her loose in 1955, it was a shock. I remember her telling me that MGM did everything for her except put the wedding rings on her finger. She didn't know how to do such simple tasks as making a hotel or plane reservation—the studio had always done that for her. She felt like an orphan.

At that time, she was married to Lex Barker, remembered as the guy who succeeded Johnny Weissmuller as Tarzan. Lana and I got to be pretty friendly, and there was the suggestion that she was interested in me. It might have happened, but I liked Lex and didn't want to intrude on their marriage.

The word around Hollywood was that Lana was a semi-nymphomaniac, and that might have been true. She did like to have a good time when she wasn't working. She drank, and even though she was never an alcoholic, she aged at a faster rate than was necessary. When she was forty, she looked fifty, and when she was fifty she looked sixty.

But Lana was *fun*. She had humor, she had energy, and she was always looking for the brightness in life. Lana would invite me to her parties, and I grew to adore her. Johnny Stompanato once asked me for Lana's phone number, but I managed to dodge that particular (literal) bullet. He got the number from somebody else and moved right in on her.

Lana once told me that she didn't like sex anywhere near as much as she liked romance—the candlelight, the soft music, the seduction. I think it was true for her, and for a lot of women. And if you think about it from the point of view of a female movie star, it makes perfect sense: They're hit on all the time—everybody wants something from them.

There has always been a very predatory attitude about women in the industry. Once, when I was preparing to leave the country to make a movie, I asked the director if he was going to take a cruise ship overseas.

"No," he said. "All the best pussy flies." I've never forgotten the remark, and the unpleasant edge it contains. It bothered me at the time, and it bothers me even more now that I have three daughters.

Even if people aren't after women stars for sex, they're after them for their time, their name on the dotted line. Rarely are they pursued for their value as people.

Think about what a burden it must be to have to own every room you walk into. And even greater than that, to worry about what the close-ups reveal—every day that ticks by makes it that much more difficult to sustain the illusion of youth. That's why cameramen of that era always used some level of diffusion when shooting women, unless the story mandated that the actress in question had a scene in a drunk tank. One cameraman told me that Tallulah Bankhead told him to shoot her "through a Navajo blanket," and she was only half kidding. Tallulah drank—a lot—and she needed all the help she could get.

To counter the pressure they faced from the industry and from themselves, many of the actresses adopted a businesslike brusqueness, while some had much harder shells—a don't-fuck-with-me-boys attitude. Survival mechanisms, pure and simple.

So many actresses wind up marrying their agent or their bodyguard—for protection, either psychological or literal. Of course, such unions can come apart quickly when the woman asks her agent/husband for advice about which film to do, and the recommended film bombs. Then the trust begins to falter, because the protection the actress imagined she was getting falters. And the cycle starts all over again.

A lot of the actresses I knew married men who were on a lower social or economic level than they were, because they were the guys who reacted to them in an honest and open way. That might help explain Elizabeth Taylor's final husband, whom she met in rehab, a choice that would otherwise have seemed evidence of temporary derangement.

So it was that Lana gravitated toward a guy who seemed to know it all—the gangster Johnny Stompanato. When Lana's daughter Cheryl Crane stabbed him to death, the newspapers went berserk; Lana's life had become inseparable from Lana's movies. She made more films after the scandal, and some of them were quite successful: *Imitation of Life* was probably the biggest, and the best, although it makes veiled reference to the Stompanato case. Lana plays an actress who wants her daughter to have the best of everything, but is too busy with her career to actually give her much attention.

Lana kept making movies well into the 1970s, played around with television a little, and then seemed to enjoy not working. It's not a surprise; she'd been supporting herself since shortly after she hit puberty. I rather like what Adela Rogers St. Johns said about Lana: "Let's not get mixed up about the real Lana Turner. The real Lana Turner is Lana Turner. She was always a movie star and loved it. Her personal life and her movie life are one."

But why shouldn't she have loved it? She was a gambler's child, tossed out into the world without any sense of personal identity beyond the need to survive. And survive she did. Sometimes messily, sometimes gloriously, but she lived a star and died a star. That is how she wanted to be remembered, and it is how she *is* remembered. Add to that her immense kindness and generosity as a person. Put it all together and in my book that makes Judy Turner's life a far greater success than she ever could have imagined at Hollywood High.

Like any other period, the 1950s had its good points and its bad. The bad points were somehow more obvious. For instance: the blacklist, that period when even nominal liberals had their careers destroyed or imperiled because of their politics. I know all about it: When my picture *Prince Valiant* opened, it got picketed because the man who wrote it, Dudley Nichols, was a liberal, or, as they're called now, a progressive. In fact, the picture should have been picketed because of the wig I had to wear. Had anybody asked, I would have been happy to organize the protest.

Dudley Nichols was never a Communist, never even close to being one, and everybody in the movie business knew it, which is probably why he managed to keep working. But he was seriously threatened by the American Legion's picketing.

The 1950s were also a period that witnessed a more openly erotic approach by female stars. Marilyn Monroe would never have been accepted in the 1940s, even though there was a healthy amount of self-parody in her image. I always thought Marilyn helped herself to aspects of Mae West's personality, but instead of Mae's self-awareness, Marilyn pretended to obliviousness. The characters she played were usually unaware of their attributes, even as they were flaunting them.

Contrary to general belief, the great sea change in the impact of female beauty was not really due to the easing up of censorship and the gradual increase in nudity, first in films coming from Europe, and later in domestic movies. Rather, it was the product of a technical development: the widespread adoption of color. Great stars like Greta Garbo, or, for that matter, Norma Shearer, existed in a black-and-white world, and it served them well because that was all there was.

But when color came in in a big way in the 1950s, when you could see the creamy complexion, the green-blue eyes, and flaming lips of stars like Ingrid Bergman, comparatively decorous black and white seemed archaic, sexually speaking. Color *eroticized* women, and it freed up male fantasies. It also enabled actresses to emphasize an aggressive sexuality that black and white had only hinted at. Certainly, Marilyn in black and white had about half the impact of Marilyn in color, up to and including *Some Like It Hot*.

And despite the stylization of color—red in the movies was invariably redder than red in real life—it also made the movies seem more real, continuing a series of innovations that had moved the art from the silent days. Sound gave the movies dialogue and natural sounds, water rushing, car motors revving, guns firing—all of which made the movies seem more a depiction of actual reality, even if the plots were outright fantasy.

Color reflected the way we actually see the world, while the influence of European actresses like Anna Magnani, Sophia Loren, Brigitte Bardot, and Gina Lollobrigida also helped. Sophia was beautiful, of course, but she was also *real*, as was Magnani. These were women of intense flesh and blood—magnificently so.

But at the same time color made it more difficult for older actresses who had built their careers on their glamour and beauty, because it was harder to hide their age in color than it had been in black and white. Loretta Young only made a few color movies, and she liked it that way. Her move into television meant she could stay in a black-and-white medium, which is yet another reason why the movies began moving resolutely toward color throughout the decade—it was a selling point, just as expensive locations and widescreen spectacle were. They were all things you couldn't get on TV.

Some actresses reflected this trend more than others. Audrey Hepburn always seemed real in spite of the fact that she wore Givenchy because she embodied a strong emotional reality. So often there was a sadness about Audrey. Marilyn was a fantasy; Audrey was real. Both glorious; both transcendent.

THE SIXTIES

The 1960s were a tumultuous time. Standards that had been around for a hundred years were overturned in the course of a decade, and that was reflected in the faces of the actresses who became popular in the era. You had movie stars who were, frankly, not beautiful by traditional movie standards. Actresses like Barbra Streisand and Mia Farrow couldn't help but make you conscious of what women had gone through and the rejections they'd had to endure. The message that their popularity sent was that movies were now much more inclusive than they had been even twenty years earlier. Then, the marquees of movie theaters across America might as well have read "Only the Beautiful Need Apply." But in the 1960s it became obvious that looks were less important than talent or drive.

This was not a completely novel development—Joan Crawford had projected many of the same qualities thirty years earlier, as had Bette Davis—but it was unusual. Most of the stars of that era made a point of not bringing their personal sadness to their work. Norma Shearer, Norma Talmadge, and Barbara Stanwyck all had tough childhoods, but on the screen they conquered the obstacles life placed in their way.

To a great extent that also describes their adult lives—never overlook the motivating force of success stories in the psychology of actresses. If their marriages or their relationships with their children were compromised to one extent or another, they invariably chose movies with happier endings than life offered.

These women flourished at a time when women in the world usually had limited options. They could be teachers, secretaries, or nurses.

Doctors or lawyers were mostly men. Yes, the best and brightest could bulldoze their way into careers in law or medicine, but that happened infrequently.

My sister was typical of her generation. She had five kids and was basically relegated to feeding them, wiping their bottoms, and raising them. In the 1960s, women said to hell with that, and thank God they did. It opened up the world to tens of millions of them.

One thing I've learned in my long life is that you can't put the genie back in the bottle. Once earned—or seized—freedom is impossible to roll back, and today we have women governors, senators, and prime ministers all over the world, and nobody thinks anything of it. Even fifty years ago, this would have been inconceivable.

As society began to change, so did Hollywood, but for a long time it wasn't sure in which direction to go. The 1950s were a time when Marilyn Monroe, Elizabeth Taylor, Audrey Hepburn, and Doris Day were huge stars, and four more dissimilar women can hardly be imagined. You might even say that Audrey and Doris amounted to a rejection by half the audience of what Marilyn and Elizabeth represented to the other half of the audience.

For a long time in the 1950s, producers tried to hedge their bets by hiring actresses who had some or most of the same qualities that reigning stars did. For instance, Pier Angeli looked a little like Audrey Hepburn, so they cast her in the same wistful roles.

20th Century Fox signed up Joan Collins in the hope that she'd become another Elizabeth Taylor—she had the same sultry accoutrements and sensual quality. That's pretty much what happened, but it took more than twenty years before Joan achieved her imperious apotheosis on *Dynasty*.

Joan had attended the Royal Academy of Dramatic Art and had been in the business since she was nine years old. She was always accomplished and always a pro. She made a lot of pictures at Fox, usually playing a sexpot—*The Girl in the Red Velvet Swing, Rally 'Round the Flag, Boys!* We made a picture together called *Stopover Tokyo*, which at least one critic referred to as *Stopover Acting.* We became more than co-workers for a time. I was falling in love with her, but I could tell something was holding Joan back. Shortly afterward, Natalie and I fell in love. A little while later, I introduced Joan to Anthony Newley, whom she began keeping company with.

Later, after Natalie and I divorced, I decided to get out of Hollywood and move to Italy. I had three reasons: my busted marriage, my career, and the fact that I had always loved Italy. I invited Joan to come with me. She thought about it and finally told me, "I'd rather stay in England." She went off and married Tony and had her daughter; I went off and married Marion and had my daughter Katie before remarrying Natalie. (Joan also had a daughter named Kate.)

So everything transpired as it was meant to.

Joan and I have been friends for more than sixty years. She's been up, and she's been down, but she always manages to climb up off the canvas where life occasionally deposits all of us. She was a terrific girl, and now she's a terrific woman, with an admirable character—and more talented than her years of playing voluptuous, over-the-top characters would lead you to think. But you know something? Nobody could play voluptuous, over-the-top characters better than Joan.

During this period, they were making better movies in Europe than they were in America. Federico Fellini had directed *La Dolce Vita* and was about to begin *8½*, Michelangelo Antonioni was starting to make his presence known, and even the low-end spaghetti Westerns had more energy and flair than you got in American pictures with similar stories and budgets.

I wanted to advance my career, which at that point was not in great shape. I didn't lack for ambition; I was very interested in working with Brigitte Bardot, the hottest thing on two legs at that time, or Alida Valli, an actress who never had the career she should have but who I thought had everything going for her. She had made a big initial splash in *The Paradine Case* and *The Third Man*, but her innate reserve made her seem a little too severe for American audiences. She spent most of her career in Europe. She was terribly underrated.

I never worked with either Bardot or Valli, but I did work with Sophia Loren, so I can't complain. Sophia was one of the first actresses I acted with in Europe, which is a hell of a way to get to know a continent. I loved her as a woman and adored her as a person—she was then as she is now: completely honest and forthright. The film was called *The Condemned of Altona* and it was directed by Vittorio De Sica, one of cinema's giants.

Vittorio was very hands on, and I mean that literally. He would come out from next to the camera, and show you where to stand, when to move. He would position your head to catch the light that he wanted. Sometimes he would even offer line readings. If he was directing Sophia, he would show her how to make an entrance by swinging his hips with a feminine flourish that was actually kind of charming, not to mention funny.

Some actors hate that kind of direction, which can reduce you to the level of a puppet, but I honestly didn't mind. Blake Edwards sometimes did the same thing, as did Lubitsch, and they all managed to sustain an actor's individuality. Besides, I had seen *The Bicycle Thief* and *Umberto D.* and been shattered by them; I figured De Sica knew more about making a De Sica film than I did.

Vittorio had the kind of fatherly, exuberant personality that is very attractive to actors, who are usually looking for approval. He had a way of guiding you that was completely noncritical. And he helped me with my vocal production, which was a minor problem for me at that point. He suggested a professor of voice named Scurri in Rome who specialized in coaching opera singers, and who helped me lower my tone and add some resonance.

Of course, Vittorio had created Sophia, not as a star, but as an actress. He directed her in *Two Women*, which won her the Oscar for Best

Actress, as well as *Yesterday, Today and Tomorrow* and a slew of other fine pictures.

I was in love with Sophia before we started the picture. Honestly, I never knew a man who met her who didn't fall for her. Making *The Condemned of Altona* with her only made me love her more. Sophia was a highly prepared actress; she had memorized the script and had ideas of her own, but would happily incorporate any advice Vittorio gave her. She *worshipped* him. I honestly believe if he had told her to dangle by a rope from a helicopter five hundred yards above the Coliseum she would have done it, and then told the pilot to fly higher in order to make the shot better.

You can judge the personality of a star by how she treats people whom she doesn't have to be nice to—the crew, for instance. Sophia treated everybody as a friend, and the crew adored her, but then kindness could have been her middle name.

Sophia was very powerful in a room; like the great stars of the era of Hollywood that I grew up watching, you always knew she was there, knew a star had entered the room even if your back was turned. There was a sudden rustling in the air, a sense of electricity. Not every actor or actress has that inner light; Joanne Woodward, for instance, was like Marilyn Monroe—she could turn it off anytime she wanted and disappear into the wallpaper.

Sophia's husband, Carlo Ponti, was very involved in the production, as he was with all of Sophia's films. Many people didn't put a great deal of stock in the marriage; Carlo was much older, bald, and pear shaped. Nobody could understand why she would choose a spouse like that when she could have had any man in the world.

I had learned that a couple of years earlier, Sophia had an affair with Cary Grant while making *The Pride and the Passion* for Stanley Kramer. She wasn't married to Carlo at the time, although they did have an understanding. She overwhelmed Cary, and he insisted she be cast opposite him in a charming comedy called *Houseboat*.

Sophia Loren

While it lasted, it was a wonderful thing for Cary.

He wanted to marry her, but she dodged him and married Carlo instead. I can see you shaking your head, but remember, she already had the bond with Carlo, and who can truly comprehend the love that exists between other people? Never underestimate emotional needs, and Carlo was already a powerful producer with eyes and ears in both the European and American markets. Carlo adored her, and Carlo protected her, which she needed. Her childhood had been one of deprivation and sorrow during and after World War II, and he gave her the security she needed.

After watching them respond to each other, I understood that the relation was not one of father and daughter but genuinely one of husband and wife. She was extremely loyal to him, and devoted to their children.

As for Cary, from the very occasional references he would make about Sophia, it was clear that he had been overcome by her. It took him a long time to get over her, as it would any man.

Sophia asked me to escort her to the Milan premiere of *The Condemned of Altona*. The response was excellent, but Fox was very nervous about the movie, as it was a thinly veiled depiction of the Krupp dynasty. The studio recut the movie for the American market and the picture failed, but Vittorio's original version was quite good. I remain proud and grateful to have worked with such a great artist.

In 2014, I was invited to Sophia's eightieth birthday party, which was to be held in Mexico City, but I was working at the time and couldn't get away. I called her shortly afterward to wish her a belated happy birthday. She closed the conversation by saying, "I love you, Robert!"

Darling Sophia, believe me when I say that the feeling is mutual.

The most enduring of the films I made in Europe is undoubtedly *The Pink Panther*, which Blake Edwards, Peter Sellers, and David Niven turned into a classic comedy. The female lead opposite David Niven was the beautiful, tragic Capucine. Cappy was an exquisite creature, with cheekbones that seemed to rise to the elevation of the Chrysler Building. Her looks indicated her first profession—in her youth she had been a haute couture model. Cappy was a very funny woman who later appeared in an episode of *Hart to Hart* with me. My kids adored her because she was so much fun.

When we made *The Pink Panther*, Cappy was the mistress of Charles Feldman, who was my agent and who tried very hard to make her a movie star. Charlie cast her in *North to Alaska* opposite John Wayne and Stewart Granger, and a bunch of other pictures. For whatever reason, the public never quite took to her. Perhaps she was a little too aristocratic in her looks, or the delightful aspects of her personality never quite came across on film.

Cappy was a manic-depressive, and when she went into her dark moods, nothing could get her out—she would become practically catatonic. She attempted suicide more than once. Audrey Hepburn told me about how she and her partner Rob Wolders saved Cappy's life after she tried to kill herself in Switzerland. They got her to the hospital, and when they went to visit her, she asked them, "Why did you bring me back?"

After the affair with Charles Feldman ran its course, Cappy was with Bill Holden for a while, but Bill had his own issues and wasn't going to be able to help Cappy. Today, of course, there are numerous medications that might have helped.

What I do know is that in 1990, Cappy leapt off the patio of her eighth-floor apartment in Switzerland. Her only survivors were her three cats. She was a gracious, elegant woman who deserved much more out of life than she got.

While I worked with a lot of actresses during this era, most of whom were special ladies, I wasn't crazy about my experience with Raquel Welch, but then a lot of people have said the same thing. The picture we did together was called *The Biggest Bundle of Them All*, and throughout the production she was unprofessional—she practically gave Edward G. Robinson a heart attack with her inability to show up on time.

The odd thing was that I had met her years before, when she was working as a ball girl at a tennis tournament in La Jolla. Years later, she became a pinup girl and made *One Million Years B.C.*, costarring with a lot of stop-motion animated dinosaurs courtesy of Ray Harryhausen. The animation was first rate, but all anybody could talk about was the way Raquel looked in her animal-skin costumes.

A star was born.

The Biggest Bundle of Them All was produced by Josef Shaftel and Sy Stewart and directed by Ken Annakin, and was shot all over France and Italy. I became good friends with Ken and his wife, Pauline. Between the locations and the cast (Eddie Robinson, Vittorio De Sica, Godfrey Cambridge), it should have been a lot of fun to make, but Raquel turned it into the equivalent of an eight-week-long proctology exam.

The film was a lighthearted caper movie about a group of goofballs who try to make a killing by kidnapping a famous gangster and holding him for ransom. It was precisely the same plot as the Sam Spiegel movie *The Happening,* and that was no coincidence; Shaftel had been in someone's office at Columbia where he had picked the script of *The Happening* off a desk, read it, and liked it so much that he decided to make his own knockoff version at MGM. (Isn't the movie business glamorous? Isn't it fun?)

This obvious plagiarism naturally aroused the ire of Columbia, and for a time a lot of lawyers were busily amassing billable hours. The end result was that MGM held our picture back while *The Happening* was released. To the best of my knowledge, nobody ever noticed the fact that the plot of our picture was identical to Spiegel's, which was a commercial disappointment in the bargain.

The truly funny thing about the entire episode was that Sam Spiegel was widely known to be one of the least ethical people in the business— if Sam owed you money, years would drift by until you got it back, and then the only way to recover it was to sue him, which took years more. The result was that Sam had the use of your money for a very long time before he had to fork it over.

The fact that Sam was finally getting a taste of his own medicine aroused no little amount of schadenfreude. With some producers, a handshake was all you needed; with others, you had to get it in writing, and with a few others, you'd best get your money in advance. With Sam, you were going to need a contract *and* a battery of Philadelphia lawyers *and* a few phone calls from the Mob.

A few years ago, I read Raquel's book *Beyond the Cleavage* and I was very impressed. She had obviously learned and grown a great deal in the intervening years. I gave copies of the book to all my daughters.

INTERMISSION II

Both at the time and in my memory the years in Europe were golden. I encountered Marion, who was living there with her two sons, Peter and Josh, whom I immediately adored.

During one vacation Marion and I took, we were traveling by ferry when I met a little girl, several years old, whom I amused by making faces. A woman named Carmel Myers and her husband were also on-board and noticed me. Carmel came over to tell me how much she liked my work in the movies, and that began a friendship. (There's nothing like admiration to win over an actor.)

I can hear what you're thinking: Carmel *who?*

Carmel Myers had been a star in silent movies, including D. W. Griffith's *Intolerance*, a part she got because Griffith had sought some advice from her father, who happened to be a well-known rabbi in Los Angeles. The rabbi didn't want any money in return for his help, but did ask if Griffith could perhaps find a part for his daughter.

That was the start of a considerable film career for Carmel, culminating in her performance in the original 1925 version of *Ben-Hur*, in which she seduced Ramon Novarro.

I had never seen her films, but I remembered my mother talking about her, so I was pleased to meet her. She was a very lively, bright, interesting person with a wide range of interests, of which movies were only one. Carmel's career had slowed with the onset of talkies, then stopped entirely, but she was an unusual woman. She figured that if the movies didn't want her, the business world would, and by the time we met in the early 1960s she was quite successful in the fragrance business.

She asked me if I would be the face of a new men's cologne she was bringing to market. I liked her, so I said yes. She hired LeRoy Neiman to do a portrait of me to use in the advertising campaign. The cologne came on the market and did just fine.

Years later, I was working on a television project with Glen Larson, who had produced both *It Takes a Thief* and *Switch*. Glen referred to me as his good-luck charm, and always cast me in his pilots because he believed my presence would ensure their success. When the Neiman painting of me came on the market, Glen bought it. Years later, when Jill St. John and I got married, Glen gave it to me as a wedding gift.

Today that portrait hangs in my office in Aspen. Whenever I look at it, I think of that delightful woman I met on a ferry ride in Italy, and the good fortune that has often graced my life. And of my friend Glen, who left us far too soon.

The thing about Hollywood and its extensions—Beverly Hills, Bel-Air, Holmby Hills, the San Fernando Valley, and the rest—is that they're essentially all part of a working town. The opportunities for socializing were more or less limited to the weekends. But a place like Palm Springs was different; people who had houses there went there not to work but to enjoy the weather and the idleness.

I lived there with Marion, and for a time with Natalie after we re-married. Our daughter Courtney was born there. Frank Sinatra had a place there as well, and Nat and I were over at his house on a regular basis. It was a time when Natalie and I rediscovered each other and our love, so it's very precious in my memory. And it's also a time when we made some friends we might not have made back in Hollywood.

Lucille Ball, for instance. I played a lot of golf with Lucy's husband, Gary Morton, who had a good game. Gary was the right man at the right time for Lucy. He was very loving and attentive, and she needed that—she had been very bruised by her marriage to Desi Arnaz.

Desi was a good guy, quite smart, but he was also a Latin male who wanted to enjoy the perquisites traditionally expected by Latin males. There are Hollywood wives who are well aware of that predilection and turn their heads away; they bask in the public image of the happy couple, and they also enjoy the perks that come from being married to a star.

But Lucy was a star in her own right, and a bigger one than Desi, whose gift for business exceeded his talent for performing. Lucy was similar to Janet Leigh in that she couldn't accept rampant infidelities. She divorced Desi and eventually married Gary, who had been a good nightclub comic. When he wasn't golfing, Gary also served as the executive producer of Lucy's TV shows.

I found Lucy to be a joy. I never worked with her, but I knew people who did, and some of them weren't exactly enthralled. She was demanding, a perfectionist, and she was one of those comics who didn't feel the need to be on all the time; when she wasn't working, she wasn't particularly funny. She was, instead, analytical.

But when she was in Palm Springs, she was on vacation, and reveled in her time off. She would climb on her motor scooter and ride down Highway 111 to our house. She didn't wear a helmet, and her red hair would blow wildly in the wind as she breezed down the road.

She fell in love with my daughter Katie. She loved the way Katie looked, she loved the way Katie acted, she loved the way Katie thought. She became Katie's unofficial godmother. What struck me about Lucy at the time, and even more in retrospect, was how sincerely interested she was in other people. This is not a common trait in show business; actors and actresses spend most of their time obsessing about their own appearance or their careers, or how other actors and actresses might affect their careers. We're always either looking in the mirror or over our shoulder.

If Lucy had ever had that quality, it wasn't apparent when I knew her. She knew what she had accomplished professionally and she was comfortable with it, which is not to say she was complacent. Work was her life, and she only stopped working when the audience began to turn away from her, first in *Mame,* in which she was completely miscast, and finally in her last TV series, which was a quick failure—an experience with which she was unfamiliar. Knowing her, it had to have been extraordinarily difficult for her to accept.

As Lucy's career was slowing down, mine was heating up, and in her later years I rarely saw her because I was working all the time. But I'll never forget Lucille Ball on her Vespa, hair tousled by the wind, coming to see my daughter with a look of pure love on her face.

Lucy was a friend; Ina Claire was more of an acquaintance. The name Ina Claire doesn't resonate today the way it once did. She made only about ten movies, the most famous of which was *Ninotchka*, in which she plays the grand duchess and has a great scene with Garbo.

But in her day, Ina Claire was one of the great theatrical comediennes, sort of a female Rex Harrison. She had impeccable technique and a knack for high comedy that never turned sentimental. She worked in plays by writers like S. N. Behrman and was a theatrical eminence alongside Katharine Cornell, Alfred Lunt, and Lynn Fontanne. Unlike them, she retired early, in 1954.

Ina married three times, the strangest one being to John Gilbert, one of the great romantic idols of silent movies, who was supposedly doomed in the talkies by how he spoke. Actually, there was nothing wrong with his voice; it was a lot like David Niven's, but it was not what the audience expected him to sound like. The legend of his supposedly bad voice refuses to die. I've occasionally wondered if Gilbert married Ina in the hopes of getting some vocal lessons that would save his career. In any case, the marriage lasted little more than a year, while Ina continued her theatrical career for another couple of decades.

She lived down the road from me in Palm Springs, and I must say I was surprised when she accepted an invitation to our house. Ina was charming, of course, but very much a *grande dame*—elderly, slightly infirm, and very dignified. A visiting duchess.

The theater in which Ina had achieved fame was already a thing of the past when I came to know her, and it reminded me of how unforgiving show-business fame can be, especially if you focus on a transient form like the theater.

Movies and TV go on forever—only the delivery system changes. Theater is a matter of memory. As soon as the curtain comes down, and when those people who were entranced by the performance die, so do the performers. Then, they're just names on a page, like Ina Claire's is today . . . except in my memory.

When I came back to America in 1964 after three years in Europe, I felt revived. I'd made some excellent pictures, and I'd found a ready-made family with Marion and her two boys. My confidence, which had been badly compromised by my divorce from Natalie and the run of mediocre pictures in which I appeared at the same time, was back.

And I found that I was now perceived in a different way than I had been—the environment awaiting me was far more welcoming than it had been when I left. I felt plugged in again, and I was quickly cast in *Harper*, opposite Paul Newman and a remarkable group of actresses: Lauren Bacall, Janet Leigh, Shelley Winters, Julie Harris, and Pamela Tiffin.

The director was a man named Jack Smight, who lacked confidence; his wife was with him on the set for the entire shoot and seemed to function as a kind of security blanket. That was annoying, because a film set derives its specific temperature from the star and the director. Our director was nervous, which can make the cast and crew nervous. But Paul pretended not to notice, and his confidence spread to the rest of the cast. The reason he was confident was because William Goldman's script was tight and amusing, and the cast kept things bubbling.

Of course, there was Shelley Winters. I began this book by saying it wouldn't be a procession of negativity, but honesty compels me to say that Shelley was a difficult woman on the best of days, and a massive pain in the ass on the worst of them. She was one of those people who enjoyed conflict.

Shelley had a major career—Actors Studio, sexpot in her youth, eventually winning two Oscars for Best Supporting Actress. As her waistline expanded, she moved into character parts, usually playing vulgar, loudmouthed broads with a touch of vulnerability. She was particularly good in *Lolita* and *Next Stop, Greenwich Village*.

But Shelley enjoyed putting her co-workers on the defensive. After a rehearsal, she'd eye another actor and say, "Is that the way you're going to do it?" Sometimes she'd even reblock the scene: "Don't stand there, stand over here." Jack Smight, who was just trying to get through the picture, would pretend he didn't see or hear Shelley usurping his job.

Angie Dickinson became a star when she made *Rio Bravo* with Duke Wayne and Dean Martin in 1959. She was an incredibly sensual woman, the complete package, with a great figure and legs, and a wonderful manner.

You could say the same things about dozens of other girls who make an impact on Hollywood in any given year, but you can count the number of them who are able to assemble careers that last forty and fifty years on one hand. Angie was one of those women.

The reason she was able to do so is, most obviously, because she's a total professional when the camera is on. There's no such thing as a bad Angie Dickinson performance, and she proved that in good movies (*Ocean's 11, Point Blank*) and bad, and on television, where she had such a great success in *Police Woman* and in many other projects, including *Pearl*, a miniseries we did together.

She's also a joy to be around. As my mother used to say, Angie is good people—loving and supportive, and more interested in the success of the overall project than in her own. You never caught Angie arguing with a cameraman about the lighting or a designer about her costumes. She's a selfless person.

When Angie and her husband, Burt Bacharach, had a daughter who was emotionally compromised, it was Angie who stepped up and raised her. Then and later, Burt's life was his music, but Angie's life was that child. Eventually the girl committed suicide. It was the worst nightmare imaginable, but Angie survived it and remains a powerful force for good in anything she does.

As far as I'm concerned, Angie was the Nordic equivalent of Elizabeth Taylor—gorgeousness personified, and one of the finest women I've ever known.

Ah, Elizabeth. After I got some traction in the movies, I got to know her in a more than passing fashion, and she just knocked me out. She had also knocked me out when I was just a green kid, but I wasn't in a position to do anything about it.

Some people vote for Ava Gardner, but I think Elizabeth was the most beautiful woman of her time. Perhaps Elizabeth's self-confidence made the difference; Ava never considered herself very talented, and I think that affected some of her choices. But Elizabeth moved through life with bravado, with gusto; she understood that life has to be seized or it can dribble away, and seize it she did.

Elizabeth's father ran an art gallery inside the Beverly Hills Hotel, so getting into the movies as a child actress via MGM was not a huge leap. Buying Impressionist art was one of the ways movie people invested their money, and Francis Taylor's gallery was a major venue. Elizabeth never really knew much of a life outside the movie business, so she was comfortable within it to an unusual degree; she understood its weird, inbred traits, but she didn't have a lot of patience with them. She was a straight-up woman; if you told her the level truth, she'd reflect it back at you.

Elizabeth had spectacular looks, but she also had a strong internal compass. She didn't know what was right for her when it came to men—she simply tried everything—but she was very aware of what was right for her on-screen. MGM made some pretty terrible pictures with her, but she always managed to transcend the material and make the movie at least watchable, which is the greatest tribute you can pay a star of that era. Whether the movies themselves were good or bad, her stardom remained unscathed. So did her personal impact.

When I produced *There Must Be a Pony* in 1986 as a vehicle for Elizabeth and me, I was frankly nervous; Elizabeth was always late in her everyday life, and frequently late on set when making a movie, and there wasn't enough elastic in the shooting schedule to accommodate any tardiness or illness. I had to guarantee the cost of her insurance, but I needn't have worried. She was on time every day, a model of professionalism, and she gave a very expert performance.

Elizabeth had a remarkable instinct for calibrating her acting for the camera; her movements got smaller the closer the camera got. For close-ups, she simply projected through her stunning eyes. I asked her where she had learned to do that, and she smiled and said, "Monty."

I should have known. Along with Mike Todd and Richard Burton, Montgomery Clift was one of the great loves of her life. If Monty hadn't been gay, I have no doubt he and Elizabeth would have married and raised stunning children. As it was, she had to be satisfied with being his devoted friend.

In most respects, Monty was an unlucky man; he was possibly the most naturally gifted actor of his generation, with an element of the romantic that Brando didn't have. But Monty was undone by alcohol abuse that ramped up after a 1957 auto accident that damaged his beautiful face. His drinking was actually far more damaging to his looks, but the accident was what he fixated on. Monty was only forty-five when he died from a heart attack, and whether the loss was greater to the movies or to Elizabeth is a matter of opinion. I know that she grieved for him for the rest of her life. Elizabeth had a major impact on my emotional life. I adored her as a woman and respected her greatly as an actress. The opportunity of having her in my life still moves me.

In 1959, I made a movie with Bing Crosby and Debbie Reynolds called *Say One for Me*. Bing had reached that stage in his career when it was believed that he could no longer carry a movie by himself, so he had to be paired off with younger performers, which, in this case, included me and Debbie.

Elizabeth Taylor

I can't say that the casting helped much. The experience of making the movie and getting to know Bing was considerably more interesting than the movie itself, but show business can be like that.

For Debbie and me it was Old Home Week. I first met her around 1950 at a party when we were running around Hollywood trying to learn how to be movie stars. She was a lower-middle-class kid, and she was determined not to be lower middle class for a minute longer than she had to be. She had very definite ideas about marriage, about children, and about career. There was no way she was going to be anything other than successful.

Debbie came from Texas, where her father had worked on the railroad. When I met Debbie, the family lived in Burbank in a very unprepossessing house, and she played the French horn at Burbank High. She entered a local beauty contest and won, and at that point her talent consisted of lip-synching to a Betty Hutton record. That got her a movie contract, but what kept her in the business was her willingness to work.

Debbie never expected to be handed anything for free, and she never forgot where she came from. When she started making money, she built a big pool in the backyard of her parents' house, a pool that was damn near the size of the house itself. She would invite over neighbors, as well as her friends in show business, to swim anytime they wanted.

I escorted Debbie to the premiere of *Singin' in the Rain*, the movie that really started her off as a movie star. In fact, I had taken her out a few times while she was shooting the film, and she told me that she had a hard time walking because her feet were bleeding—Gene Kelly was a nice guy and a good friend, but he was a perfectionist and wasn't about to lower his professional standards for anyone, especially not for a nineteen-year-old kid whom he had to teach to dance. Debbie was crazy about me, and I loved her. In fact, she threw a twenty-first birthday party for me.

There was a time when I loved Debbie, but I never quite tumbled all the way. I've always been a little more casual about life than she was, and I wasn't sure we'd mesh well together.

Her attitude toward MGM was similar to my attitude toward Fox—

our employment wasn't servitude, but a God-given opportunity. She was getting free acting, singing, and dancing lessons. If she paid attention and worked hard, she could become expert in all those areas, an all-around entertainer hirable into old age. She was being featured in movies with show-business greats, which in and of itself constituted a compounded opportunity. She was getting a good salary that eventually became a great salary.

What was not to like?

Debbie could sing, and Debbie could dance, and Debbie could also act. She was by far the best thing in Paddy Chayefsky's *The Catered Affair*, which featured Bette Davis and Ernest Borgnine. Her costars were both projecting, both *acting*, while Debbie was *being*—yearning and sad, emotions she had certainly experienced in life.

Debbie has always been one of those people striving to make lemonade out of the most bitter lemons, and there have been some doozies in her life. Bad marriages—I know she paid off Harry Karl's debts, which were considerable—and bad business decisions, including a bankruptcy when she opened a hotel in Las Vegas that was too far off the Strip to get traffic.

For Debbie, the hotel was primarily an opportunity to display the astonishing collection of Hollywood memorabilia she'd built up over the years, so she sold off the gambling license. That might not have been the greatest financial option, but it was typical of her integrity. The hotel became a place where other performers would drop in after they'd done their shows for the night. She was always there, greeting people and encouraging them to have a good time.

Whatever landed on her doorstep, Debbie always managed to bounce back—the Unsinkable Debbie Reynolds. Her honorary Oscar in 2015 was a recognition of her talent, but also of her spirit.

A few years ago she auctioned off her collection of Hollywood costumes for tens of millions of dollars. I know that she did it with mixed feelings—she had always wanted to open a lavish Hollywood Museum, but nobody else was as interested in that prospect as Debbie, and the value of the costumes had escalated to such an extent that she had no choice but to take advantage of their market value.

One of the joys of Debbie is her industriousness. Besides her costume collection, she and Ruta Lee founded the Thalians, a great show-business charity. Because she's been around for so long, Debbie has lately been taken for granted, somewhat in the same way that Mickey Rooney had been. A performer whose career has endured for sixty-odd years, or, in Mickey's case, ninety years, can fade simply because of overfamiliarity.

When Albert Brooks couldn't get Nancy Reagan to star with him in *Mother*, he hired Debbie, and she was remarkable in the title role— steely and tough and unyielding and funny and, underneath it all, endearing, just as she was playing Liberace's mother in *Behind the Candelabra*. If she was overlooked in the latter performance, it was because between the heavy makeup and a convincing Polish accent— Debbie has a great ear for voices—most people didn't know it was her.

I respect her talent, but what I particularly adore about Debbie is her gallantry. Like everybody else, she can get depressed, but she never lets the audience see her that way. When the light hits her, she's *on*, and the audience is going to have a great time, or Debbie's going to discover the reason why not. She wants to make people happy, which is why she's one of the great show-business professionals.

NATALIE

People often ask me what Natalie Wood was like, and that's a question that's difficult to answer succinctly. She was a complicated woman, which is just one of the reasons I loved her. You could never really plumb Natalie's depths.

For one thing, she was not calm by nature, which I attribute to her childhood. From her earliest days, Natasha Gurdin—her real name—was the family breadwinner. The story of Natalie's discovery traces back to Ann Rutherford, who was making a picture in Santa Rosa called *Happy Land*. The trailer Ann was using on location had been rented from Natalie's parents, and Ann met Natalie's mother when she was cleaning out the trailer. A bit later, Nat's mom managed to wangle a bit part for her daughter in the film. In the shot in which Natalie appears, she is holding an ice cream cone, and her half sister, Olga, has her other hand. The girls' mother instructed Olga to knock the ice cream cone out of Natalie's grip to make her cry—the idea being to attract the camera's attention.

Irving Pichel, who directed *Happy Land*, also made *Tomorrow Is Forever*, a film Natalie made that starred Claudette Colbert and Orson Welles. One of the reasons I loved Claudette was that she adored Natalie. Whenever I saw her, she would always talk about how gifted Natalie was as a child—a little girl, only five years old, with her hair dyed blond and a German accent, working with Claudette Colbert and Orson Welles. God-given talent.

The assistant director on *Tomorrow Is Forever* was a man named Artie Jacobson. He was going to work on *Miracle on 34th Street*, which had been cast except for the juvenile lead. That little girl had to be able to indicate that she was old for her years, and strong-minded.

One night at four in the morning, Jacobson was running over the outstanding issues that had to be addressed before the picture could begin shooting when it suddenly hit him: "Jesus God, Natasha!" He called George Seaton, who was directing *Miracle on 34th Street*, and told him all about this child prodigy who spoke English, Russian, and a smattering of other languages and had stolen a picture out from under Claudette Colbert and Orson Welles. Artie called Ann Rutherford, who told him how to get in touch with the family. George Seaton met with her, and that was that.

Within the Gurdin family, if Natalie got an acting job, she was great, everybody's darling, the apple of their eye. If she wasn't chosen, they wanted to know what the hell went wrong.

Even if she did get hired, there were stresses she hadn't bargained for. Natalie told me that on one of her early pictures, an assistant director—not Artie Jacobson—stuck her with a pin to get her to cry on camera. This sort of dehumanizing thing went on more often than you might imagine in those days. Actors—even child actors—were considered a commodity, and they were treated as such.

So, in Natalie's mind, work soon came to be equated with success. As with Barbara Stanwyck, she became more animated when she was acting; the light inside her suddenly shone brighter.

After *Miracle on 34th Street*, Natalie worked regularly with people the caliber of Stanwyck and Bette Davis. Both older actresses thought she had almost unlimited potential, which she demonstrated by doing a lot of live TV. She was working hard to open up her image from that of a conventional child actress. She signed a contract at Warner Bros., where she made *Rebel Without a Cause* with Jimmy Dean, which brought her to a different level.

By the time I met Natalie, she had already developed a tremendous ability to recognize good material, although in the early days at Warners there wasn't a lot of it to go around. Jack Warner gave her

Natalie Wood

grindhouse stuff like *Bombers B-52*—the title alone tells you what type of film it was.

Because of the quality of scripts that Jack assigned her, and an overall feeling that he didn't give her a lot of credence as anything more than a juvenile favorite, she never really trusted him. As a matter of fact, she didn't trust a lot of people; she had her own idea of what was right and wrong for her, and had faith in her own judgment.

Then and later, she approached scripts not as a reflection of her own career needs so much as an overall dramatic extension of her emotional life. Natalie would read a script with great intensity. She looked for an arc, which is actor talk for a character who goes through changes and emerges a different person at the end of the picture than they had been at the beginning. When she found a script she wanted to do, she would break it down very methodically. As much as any actress I've ever known, she had a tremendous concept of quality, not just of what was good for her.

Her family hadn't wanted her to do *Rebel Without a Cause*, but she went after it with all of her heart, which was huge, and got it.

The same thing happened with *Splendor in the Grass*, where she beat out some very fine actresses for the lead role, including Jane Fonda. The reason that Elia Kazan chose her over Fonda was that Natalie admitted to him that she was ambitious, and Fonda wouldn't. Kazan wanted an actress who wasn't afraid to be great. Natalie wanted to be great, so she was.

Before *Splendor in the Grass*, Natalie's control over her pictures was hit and miss; after *Splendor*, she had as much control as she cared to exercise. Once she had achieved a position where people listened to what she had to say, she would rely on her director for guidance until he proved he couldn't be relied upon. *Splendor* wasn't a totally great experience for her. She put herself completely in Kazan's hands, acquiesced to him. But she was slightly uneasy about the experience; on some level she felt that Kazan had tricked the performance out of her, and she resented it. She was excited to work for him, and she liked the film, but she felt that he was devious; he had agendas that he didn't let her in on.

She was great in *Splendor in the Grass*, but Warren Beatty was great in it, Pat Hingle was great in it, everybody was great in it because Kazan directed it. (For the record, my favorite performance of Natalie's is *This Property Is Condemned*.) I've always believed that at that particular stage of his career, Kazan was the best director working in America. I was on the set for most of the production, and Gadge and I liked each other immediately. We stayed friends for the rest of his life, and I've seldom met anyone who was so perpetually dissatisfied with his own accomplishments.

Gadge moved toward conflict in his art and in his life as if it were a magnet. He was *so* talented, *so* interesting. He was the best director in the world, and yet he was completely unpretentious. He'd ask, "What do you think about that scene?" and it seemed that he really did want to know what you thought.

Of course, not every movie is *Splendor in the Grass*. Natalie always felt that *Gypsy* should have been more than it was. It wasn't that Mervyn LeRoy did a bad job, but he didn't do an outstanding job, either. He was slightly passé at that point, and Natalie and I both thought the picture reflected that. LeRoy was an odd choice on Jack Warner's part, as there were far more appropriate talents available: George Cukor certainly, George Sidney or Vincente Minnelli possibly.

But Mervyn had been around Warners for years, during the 1930s and since the late 1950s. He had a cast-iron contract, and had worked in vaudeville as a young man, so Jack gave him the picture. The problem was that the core of *Gypsy* is ferocious need and frustrated ambition, and Mervyn hadn't made a picture that reflected those qualities since *I Am a Fugitive from a Chain Gang* and *Five Star Final*, thirty years earlier.

Natalie and I worked together several times, once in *All the Fine Young Cannibals* at MGM, and in the TV movies *The Affair* and *Cat on a Hot Tin Roof;* she also made a guest appearance in the pilot for *Hart to*

Hart. She was a spectacular co-worker, and my being her husband made no difference in how she treated me as a colleague—she was demanding and rightfully so. She could be high strung—when she was into the character that was all she thought about. At the production stage, her emphasis was on remaining faithful to the material and not letting it get watered down.

When Natalie became a mother, she found the absolute fulfillment she had been waiting for. Acting filled her up, and with good reason. When the camera rolls, it's exciting. Wardrobe, makeup, the crew focused on *you*, the camera moving in on *you*. Because of the intensity of the work, many people in show business have trouble adjusting, not to the work, but to life.

But to our mutual joy, Natalie was swept away by motherhood. It was a total home run for her. She was devoted to our girls. Years later, when Natalie's daughter Natasha had her own child, she had the same mothering instincts as Natalie, which moved me so deeply. Natasha named her little girl Clover, after Natalie's movie *Inside Daisy Clover*, which is one of Natasha's favorites of her mother's films. I don't think Natasha has ever taken her eyes off Clover. Her mother, my wife, would have been so proud of her daughter. The torch had been passed.

When Natalie died, I thought my life was over. Luckily, I had the help of a great many people who loved her and who loved me as well. Fred Astaire. Cary Grant. Gene Kelly. Delphine Mann. David Niven. Our children. My mother. And John Lindon, a great psychiatrist who helped. I remember he once drew a picture of a heart for me. "This much is gone," he said, gesturing to the picture. "But this much is left, and that can be enough. It *has* to be enough—for your girls and for yourself."

And that is the way it worked out—for the girls and for myself.

JILL

With many of the actresses I've written about, you can get a sense of who they really are just by attentively watching them on-screen. That won't work with Jill St. John, my last—I promise—wife.

I had worked with Jill three times before she came into my life at its lowest point. The first picture we worked on was called *Banning*, and then we were paired on a TV movie called *How I Spent My Summer Vacation*. Years later, she appeared in the pilot of *Hart to Hart*. In all these cases, our relationship was purely professional. If someone had taken me aside and told me that one day I would fall in love with her, I would have had them committed. I thought she was pleasant and a good actress, but there was no spark between us.

I didn't really get much of an insight into who she really was until years later, soon after Natalie's death. Jill had sent flowers to the house, and I called to thank her. Six or eight months later, I asked her out. She called our mutual friend Tom Mankiewicz, who was a creative consultant on *Hart to Hart*, and asked him what he thought she should do.

"Well, if you don't go out with him, someone else will," he said. You can't argue with crushing logic like that, so she accepted my invitation. And that was when I figured out that she was actually the reverse of the characters she played. Her mother had nudged her into show business and she went along grudgingly; she didn't run after movies, they ran after her.

I remember her apartment in Beverly Hills was decorated in Italian Modern, which surprised me. And then she told me, "Come to Aspen,

Jill St. John

and you'll see a whole different side of me." So I did, and I saw how Aspen was the place where Jill relaxed and allowed her authentic self to emerge. In Aspen, she blossomed in front of me. She's a Cordon Bleu chef, she's a superb gardener, she excels at skiing and handling dogs and everything in general. Whatever she undertakes, she masters.

And beyond all that, she reads everything and is ridiculously smart, one of those people who sees the endgame while other people are still mulling over their opening move.

People who know Jill only through movies like *Come Blow Your Horn* or *Diamonds Are Forever* don't have a clue. Hollywood typecast her as a sexy bombshell, and Jill got bored with that very quickly, because the gap between what she played and who she is was so vast. She is as attached to the earth as anybody I've ever met. Whether it's flowers or love, she has the ability to create an environment where things grow. She can bring the world around her to its fullest possibilities.

If somebody sent her a good script today, she'd probably do it, but she doesn't really care about acting—it doesn't fill her heart the way living in Aspen does; it doesn't satisfy her the way cooking or gardening does.

And here's my deepest truth: We've been together for more than thirty years, and I still have a sense of discovery with her every single day that accompanies an underlying feeling of security and contentment—the best of both worlds.

I owe her everything.

THE EIGHTIES (AND ON)

No discussion of the actresses I've worked with would be complete without Stefanie Powers. In my memory, there are so many ironies connected with her. Nobody wanted her for *Hart to Hart*, except for Tom Mankiewicz and me. Stefanie had had a major flop with *The Girl from U.N.C.L.E.* years before and the TV business had never forgiven her.

As for ABC, their preferences were, first, Natalie—a total non-starter, because we would have had no private life at all—and second, Lindsay Wagner. They thought the tagline "Wagner and Wagner" was just too good to pass up.

I thought they were idiots.

But Stefanie and I had worked together a few years before, and I knew that we meshed. Her timing complemented my own. Finally, it got down to my saying, "It's her, or there's no show," and since I held a lot of cards at that time, they gave in.

Irony number one.

Then we made the pilot, and Sidney Sheldon took his name off the show as the creator. It was Tom Mankiewicz who was ultimately responsible for so much of the success of that program. He rewrote Sheldon's script for the pilot, and when it went to series he ran the show.

In any case, Sheldon put his name back on the show after it became a big hit. In spite of the fact that it was widely thought to be a potential smash—Aaron Spelling and Leonard Goldberg didn't make a lot of bombs—getting it on the air was a tortuous process, but it never showed in the final product.

Irony number two.

To this day, people think that Stefanie and I were actually married, or should have been. Of all the dozens of actresses I've worked with, Stefanie is the one people most often associate with me. The truth is that the success of the show was a tribute to the mysterious nature of screen chemistry. Stefanie and I meshed beautifully as actors, but we've never had that much in common as people; we'd do the work and then go our separate ways.

Irony number three.

If you think about great screen teams, they were rarely emotionally involved. Spencer Tracy and Katharine Hepburn lived together for years, but William Powell and Myrna Loy were just friends.

I think it's entirely possible that marriage gets in the way of a successful screen pairing, simply because a husband and wife know each other too well to provoke any sense of genuine discovery.

Stefanie was always a pro—she knew the script, she did her own makeup, and she was on top of every detail, so much so that there were times when she also would have been happy to write, produce, and direct the show.

She had a sense of lilt, of humorous delicacy in her characterization, and she also had that touch of class that went with the show's premise—the flowers, the Rolls-Royce, the level of production that Aaron and Leonard gave us. I can honestly say that Stefanie never disappointed me as an actress. She was the perfect Jennifer Hart—humor, intelligence, amazing looks. She made a tremendous contribution to the series' success.

Of course, actors are helpless without good writing, and that's where Mart Crowley and Tom Mankiewicz came in. Mart had worked for Natalie when he was a young man, and he came back to work with me after his huge success with *The Boys in the Band*. Mart wrote the relationships and the patter on *Hart to Hart*, which sounds easy until you try to do it. I always pined for a pair of writers who could be the TV equivalent of Billy Wilder and Charlie Brackett, but for some

Stefanie Powers

reason writers don't like to collaborate anymore, so the plots would be done by one writer, and the dialogue by Mart.

The production process was fairly typical; we'd take seven days to make an episode, and they were long days—ten hours occasionally, twelve hours regularly. After that, we'd head home, have a meal, go over our lines for the following day, and go to bed.

One-hour TV shows devour your life, so it's mandatory that the working conditions be as stress free as possible. You don't want people around you who impede the mechanics of the process. If someone on the crew wasn't happy, I would talk to them once. If the person was still a problem, they were gone. After a year or two of the show's success, writers would begin to agitate to be promoted to producers, because producers make more money, so there is always the matter of negotiating careerist jostling.

When I went back to work after Natalie died, I was so filled with anxiety. Stefanie came into my trailer and said, "You're going to be all right." And she took me by the hand and led me to the set. I don't know if I could have walked there myself. She was there for me. Leonard had closed the company down for almost a month, and when Stefanie and I appeared, the entire crew offered their warm support.

Stefanie was with Bill Holden then and until his tragic death. He introduced her to the glory of Africa, which was his great passion and which became hers. Their enthusiasm gradually grew; Bill was a great guy, a man's man and a ladies' man as well, but the two of them could clear out a room talking about zebras.

After Bill died, Tom Mankiewicz fell under Stefanie's spell and built a house next to hers in Africa, but the relationship didn't work out.

Years after *Hart to Hart* went off the air, Stefanie and I reunited for a batch of TV movies, and the chemistry was still spot on.

Now, I see Stefanie when the Museum of Broadcasting or a TV show wants to do a *Hart to Hart* reunion. Just as we did thirty years ago, when the lights switch off, we head in opposite directions, but I will always be grateful to her for the radiant personality that made our show the first-rate entertainment it was. And I will never forget her strength and kindness in the worst moments of my life.

Audrey Hepburn holds a special place in my heart, and always will. I have a picture of her as a little girl, and she had the same adorable face and nature then that movie audiences everywhere would come to love.

Audrey had the most fantastic spirit of any woman I've ever known. You can look at a picture of her when she was three years old and see Audrey clearly. I've encountered only one other woman who had that quality: Elizabeth Taylor. We all have different aspects of ourselves that we reveal, depending on circumstances. Sometimes we're soft and yielding, and sometimes quite the opposite. But Audrey had no façade; she was consistently Audrey in every aspect of her life.

And there was something else—she absorbed everything that life put in her path, and then reflected it back to the world, concentrated and doubled and transformed into beauty. The flowers that filled her house in Switzerland, the fabrics on her furniture, the fashions she wore—all combined to create a sense of a unified personality in the way that nature often does, but that is seldom found in human beings.

Beneath Audrey's surface was a sense of sadness, which I believe was caused by her sensitivity to life and to other people. She understood on a fundamental level that life is often unfulfilling at best and tragic at worst, and she carried that with her as a counterweight to the fulfillment her beauty and talent earned her. She put everything she had into UNICEF, but that was typical—if Audrey committed to something, it was with her whole heart.

I might add that Sophia Loren has some of that same sensitivity; they both grasped what you were feeling, sometimes before you did. In both cases, I think early poverty might have been the cause. Certainly, young Audrey being subjected to the Nazi invasion of Holland had a tremendous impact on her psyche.

Audrey was confronted by the impermanence and instability of the world, and that knowledge accompanied her everywhere she went, even as she tried to compensate for some of that insufficiency. Both of her marriages failed, through no fault of her own. This affected her deeply, until she found great happiness with Rob Wolders late in her life. Rob was also Dutch, and they had much in common besides their nationality.

I first met Audrey when I went to Europe to do *The Mountain* with Spencer Tracy. She was married to Mel Ferrer at the time. Mel had a good sense of humor, but could be slightly remote. I was immediately struck by Audrey's beauty, as everyone was, but her personality was every bit as attractive as her face. She was shy by nature, but tried to be open. Years later, we did a TV movie together, one of the last things she did before her death.

As an actress, Audrey knew her work. She moved her process out of the way in order to let her being come through, and it was her being that made Audrey special to the world. She was a magical presence.

In reading over this, it sounds as if I had a crush on Audrey Hepburn. Well, why should I be any different from everybody who ever worked with her? Why should I be any different from the rest of the world?

Beginning in the 1970s and continuing through the 1980s, I did more TV than film. I found that I liked the rapid pace of television, but there is a cost to speed, and that relates to the overall emotional experience of the production process.

A movie takes eight weeks, sometimes longer, so you might be working with a given actor or actress for months at a time, which means you really get to know them. It's not just a matter of the hours spent in rehearsals and the performance, there's also a lot more downtime while you're waiting for the lights, or moving from one location to another. Just having the opportunity to sit around talking to and asking

Audrey Hepburn

questions of actors I spent my youth watching was always one of the greatest perks of the business as far as I was concerned.

But TV moves very quickly—on *Hart to Hart*, I might work with guest stars for three or four days, which didn't allow for a huge amount of leisure to get to know them. But some of them do stand out in my mind. I've mentioned Joan Blondell and a few others, but I also want to pay tribute to Dorothy Lamour.

Dotty was one of those performers whom everybody liked—other actors, the crew, the front office, everybody. She had been a huge star before, during, and after World War II in South Sea movies like John Ford's *The Hurricane*, the Bob Hope and Bing Crosby Road pictures, and so forth. Her last big picture had been DeMille's *The Greatest Show on Earth* in 1952, after which she had more or less retired.

She married a man who lived in Baltimore, had some kids, and enjoyed her second career as a wife and mother. She toured in *Hello, Dolly!* and dinner theater in the 1960s and 1970s, but hadn't been doing a lot of TV or film work when she came on *Hart to Hart*, so I really had no idea what to expect.

I needn't have worried—she knew the script cold. It wasn't *The Hurricane*, but if she felt any disappointment about doing television, she didn't show it. She was still miffed about Bob and Bing; she felt they had given her short shrift over the years, and not taken her contributions to their films seriously.

If Dotty felt that she had been put on the shelf after she got to be a certain age, she didn't let it spoil her pleasure in the work she still had. When she died, her family asked me to give the eulogy for a very classy lady.

In retrospect, Dorothy Lamour's experience was symptomatic of an abiding show-business trait, one that persists even today.

As I've discussed earlier in this book, forty can be difficult for any woman, but in show business it's especially difficult. An actress like Meryl Streep, who sails into her sixties still playing the few leading parts for women of her age, is the exception; she's the American equivalent of British actresses like Vanessa Redgrave or Maggie Smith, who will work as long as they can stand up, and when they can no longer stand up will work sitting down. They're that good, and they've also formed strong, lasting bonds of affection with audiences.

And there's another issue, which is the nature of the industry itself. Audiences used to be heavily invested in their female stars because the studios themselves had invested in those actresses. They were presented with all the glorious lighting and dramatic impact possible. And the audience responded. Those backlit, erotically charged close-ups had impact. They still do.

But women aren't presented that way anymore; they seldom have that kind of erotic power, and if they do, they don't have it for long. The few real female stars are in perpetual transit from one studio to another. Stars today are actually highly paid migrant workers, or, if you prefer, independent nation-states; they have nobody to look out for their interests but themselves and the people with whom they surround themselves.

Add to that the fact that the media surrounding celebrity has never been more carnivorous than it is today, and what you have is a recipe for shortened careers. I've mentioned the brief runs that stars like Betty Hutton had, and the truncated professional life of someone like Ann Sheridan. But even then, Betty Hutton had ten good years, and Ann Sheridan had slightly more than that, runs for which a lot of modern actresses would consider bartering a child.

That underlying reality of the movie business can be summed up by the famous remark of Jean-Baptiste Alphonse Karr: The more things change, the more they remain the same.

In 1988, I did a remake of a Cary Grant/Ingrid Bergman picture called *Indiscreet*, about a middle-aged love affair. I wanted to do it with Candice Bergen, but CBS wouldn't hear of it. I kept agitating for Candy, but it got to the point where the network said they would not go forward with the project unless we dropped the idea of Candy as my leading lady.

Over and over they explained their reasoning, as if I was slightly dim: "She's an ice queen. She doesn't have a sense of humor."

So the network gave me Lesley-Anne Down, who proved to have no affinity with me or anybody else whatsoever. A year or two later, Candy got *Murphy Brown*—a CBS show, I hasten to point out—and the woman who had no sense of humor was off and running in one of the great sitcoms.

I see Candy and her husband whenever I go to New York, and she remains one of the most delightful women I've known. Had she done *Indiscreet* with me, I have no doubt that the result would have been something special. As it worked out, if you mention *Indiscreet*, people think of Cary Grant and Ingrid Bergman . . . as they should.

This is the sort of thing that makes show business so crazy, and it became just a little crazier as TV became increasingly important— eventually more important—than the movie business. Because there's more work in TV, there are many more slots for actors, so the talent pool becomes bigger. Unfortunately, so does the lack-of-talent pool, as I found out in the case of *Indiscreet*.

But quality does have a way of sustaining itself. Take Jaclyn Smith, easily one of the finest women in the business, and widely loved. Jackie is steady, humorous, a hard worker. She backed away from acting to occupy herself with business and charity work, but whenever I see her I'm glad I did. She's one of those people who's a thorough pleasure to be around—a special woman. And she can make me laugh like few people have.

Jackie came to fame and fortune on *Charlie's Angels*, on which Natalie and I had a healthy profit percentage. I got her the part in that show. She had recently worked with me on an episode of *Switch*, shot in Las Vegas. She played a cocktail waitress, and the local news station covered the scene we were shooting. We got back to the hotel, and there was a call from Dean Martin. He wanted to meet her. I told her about it, but she didn't want to go there.

Jaclyn Smith

I was impressed with her, and took her to meet Aaron and Leonard, who ended up signing her as one of the Angels.

And there are a few more unforgettable women I have to discuss before closing.

I got to know Julie Andrews through my friendship with her husband, Blake Edwards. Blake cast me in *The Pink Panther*, and we remained friends over the years. Blake and Julie had a place in Gstaad, and they hosted my family many times, usually for the holidays. There would be other close friends there—Audrey Hepburn and Rob Wolders, and Robert Loggia—God bless him—and his wife.

With Julie, as with so many of the women in this book, what you see is what you get, and that is always an amazing quality in anyone. If I had to sum her up in one word it would be *empathy*, which I think is something you're either born with or not. She's interested in the emotional and practical lives of the people she cares about, and that's reflected in a special quality of warmth that I've always been drawn to. She's always been very family oriented, with her kids as part and parcel of their parents' lives, not fobbed off on nannies.

How remarkable is Julie? I knew Blake before he met Julie, and there was a considerable difference afterward. Blake had always been a ladies' man, but that ended when he married Julie.

Seeing Julie in Gstaad was fascinating; she didn't interfere with Blake's energy—she let him set the general direction and followed along, but she also guided him, never letting things get too wild. Blake loved her, of course, but he also respected her instincts and let himself be directed by her.

And there's something else that struck me about Julie, then and now: a tremendous sense of gratitude. She knows she's talented, but she doesn't think of herself as being especially remarkable; she believes that some of her career has been a matter of pure luck and some of it has been due to the fact that people simply like her. She gives the impression that she doesn't really have any idea why that might be the case.

Consider her response when she lost her singing voice because of a botched throat operation. Julie's identity had always been based primarily on being an outstanding singer, and she woke up one day and could no longer sing. That is a devastating development. A lot of people—*most* people—would be derailed if they were suddenly unable to do what had defined them all their lives. They'd go on TV and talk about their bravery in overcoming the terrible obstacle that had been placed in their path.

Julie never did anything of the kind. She absorbed the situation, then got on with her life. If she shed any tears, they were shed in private.

Nothing defeats Julie. Nothing.

Losing Blake was bad, very bad, even though we all knew how frail he was. Blake had been an aficionado of martial arts when he was younger—the karate fights between Inspector Clouseau and "my little yellow friend" Kato in the Pink Panther movies were Blake's way of paying comic tribute to his hobby. But he had terrible back trouble for years and he had been in a wheelchair for some time before his death.

Again, Julie did her mourning in private and then briskly went about her business. She writes—a best-selling memoir, successful children's books written with her daughter Emma—and she continues to act whenever she gets the chance.

I think Julie's wrong about one thing: People love her for very good reasons, and she reflects that love back in all directions.

In so many ways, Julie is a blessed woman, and to have her in your life is a blessing in return.

Failure presents all sorts of problems. So does success. The difference is that the problems of failure are obvious, while the problems of success sneak up on you. If you're an actor, success can give you financial security, but it can also fix you in the public mind in a way that makes it nearly impossible to move on, to do anything else. What started out as success seamlessly evolves into incremental frustration.

My friend Florence Henderson illustrates this principle. Florence was a star on Broadway, in the Joshua Logan production of *Fanny*—a great show with an exquisite score by Harold Rome. She's also starred in movies (*Song of Norway*) and done good work in dozens of television shows, not to mention appearing in a smashing nightclub act. She's also sung the national anthem at the Indianapolis 500 more times than anybody else in history.

But most people only remember her for *The Brady Bunch*. Granted, this is better than not being remembered at all, and I'm sure Florence is grateful for all the opportunities she's had because of the show, but it's still locked her into a public image as the bright, ever cheerful, always competent mom negotiating the adolescent squabbles of Jan and Marcia.

Years after *The Brady Bunch*, Florence did an episode of *Hart to Hart* with me, and after that we would occasionally encounter each other around town. The more I saw her, the more I grew to respect her. Florence always had talent, but she never had it made. She was one of ten children, grew up poor, and sang at outdoor markets for spare change.

About twenty-five years ago I found myself on the same plane as Florence at a time when I could feel myself slipping into depression. Depression can involve personal issues, things like professional frustrations—that is to say external, more or less rational causes—or it can be part of your chemistry or your biorhythms and have nothing to do with any objective reality.

I had just enough experience with depression to know how crippling it can be. You can feel the fog gathering, then darkening. First it gradually obliterates your vision of the world, so that all you can see or feel is the fog, and then it moves on to your navigational skills. You can't get away.

I went over to say hi to Florence, and in the course of the conversation I told her how I was feeling, after which I complimented her on her own level of positive energy. She waved the compliment aside and said, "I've had a lot of help." And then she began telling me about a woman who had helped her through various crises through hypnosis.

I had used hypnosis once or twice before, mainly to cope with a bad case of stage fright. Florence suggested that it might very well help me forestall a full-scale bout of depression, and she gave me a referral. The trick with any medical professional is to find someone you can relate to and trust, and I immediately felt comfortable with Florence's friend Cheryl O'Neill.

Before Cheryl puts you into the hypnotic state, you talk to her about the issues that are overloading you—what you're anxious about. You're lying down, with your eyes closed and with a blanket over you. Cheryl will instruct, "Take three deep breaths. You'll feel your feet relaxing, your legs, your knees." You visualize coming down a series of stairs. When you reach the floor, you turn to the right. At that point, sometimes you drift off into something that feels like sleep, while other times you're fully conscious and aware of what's being said in the room.

After Cheryl puts you under, she addresses your issues. Sometimes after you come out of it, you can feel an immediate sense of relief, while other times it takes a little longer. After I'd been going to Cheryl for a while I found that I could hypnotize myself in order to deal with basic problems like insomnia, or even to moderate negative impulses like impatience and anger. Hypnosis has proven good for my concentration, and great for my imagination.

What I didn't realize at the time is that most analysts use hypnotism at one time or another, on one patient or another. A lot of athletes use it, especially those who need to maintain focus over a lengthy competition in which they're basically isolated, such as golfers and baseball players. I also know a number of singers who use it, not to mention actors, as completing a few minutes of usable film over an eight- or ten-hour workday requires more concentration than a lot of people can supply all by themselves.

As I've gotten to know Florence better, I've come to realize that she is a genuinely interesting woman, and very far from the character of Carol Brady. She's been knocked on her behind many times and she always gets up—the most critical character attribute if you're going to have any kind of a rewarding life.

She's a hell of a lady who made a huge difference in my own life, and an indefatigable, magnetic personality.

It seems like I've known Don Johnson forever. He used to refer to me as his good luck charm because I ran into him a day or so before *Miami Vice* got picked up by NBC and I told him the project sounded very strong. Years after, he and Melanie Griffith bought a house in Aspen, and Don and I passed the time by playing countless rounds of golf, not to mention a lot of fly fishing.

When Melanie gave birth to their daughter, Dakota, I visited them at the hospital and was the second man to hold that beautiful child. A few years later, Jill and I were invited to Don's annual Fourth of July party. Dakota was about four by that time, and when she saw us coming up the driveway, she took off running toward us. After a sprint of about fifty yards, Dakota came to a screeching halt and breathlessly asked Jill, "Where did you get that lip gloss?"

I told Don he had a serious problem.

All this is by way of explaining that our families became intertwined in a way I could never have foreseen when I worked with Melanie's mother, Tippi Hedren, in an episode of *It Takes a Thief.* It was the period after the failure of *Marnie,* when Tippi was working out her contract with Universal.

At the time, nobody at Universal really knew if there had been a relationship between Hitchcock and Tippi, but we all wondered. He had clearly been besotted with her. *The Birds* had been a great success—I think it's Hitchcock's last good picture—and despite the critical and financial failure of *Marnie,* Tippi was by far the best thing in the picture. It's such a strange movie; Sean Connery's character is actually more psychologically damaged than Tippi's, but none of the other characters seem aware of it. For that matter, neither does Hitchcock.

I knew a lot of actors who worked for Hitchcock, and, with the exception of Jimmy Stewart and Cary Grant, none of them enjoyed the experience. If you were going to act for Hitchcock, you were going to be left more or less alone. Paul Newman told me Hitchcock's attitude toward actors was "Wheel in the meat and shoot it." (Small-world department: Tom Wright, who's one of the best directors at *NCIS*, used to be a storyboard artist for Hitchcock.)

Hitchcock was beloved by Lew Wasserman. Lew gave Hitchcock his own unit at Universal, housed in his own building, and made him very wealthy. The strange thing is that both Lew and Hitchcock tended to be cold—dust could come out of their mouths.

I worked with Melanie in *Crazy in Alabama*, which was directed by Antonio Banderas, whom she married after she and Don divorced. It was the first—and only—picture directed by Antonio, and I thought he did a very creditable job. Most of my scenes were shot at the Chateau Marmont, and throughout the shoot Antonio was totally prepared. He knew what he wanted out of every line of the script and every shot. On top of that, I found him to be a kind, empathetic director, probably because he was an actor long before he began directing and knew actors' problems from the inside.

Melanie was accomplished and professional in a part that was quite a stretch for her—she played a woman who kills her husband, abandons her children (one of whom was played by Dakota), and takes off for Hollywood in search of fame and fortune, accompanied by the head of her late husband. As you can see, the title was an accurate reflection of the movie. Working with her, I realized that Melanie had a lot more on the ball than she'd been able to show professionally—she's obviously a very sexy girl and got typed early.

Melanie isn't particularly like her mother, other than the fact that they're both dreamers. Tippi presents as aristocratic, while Melanie is earthier, but they share a devotion to Tippi's great passion, the Shambala Animal Preserve.

Eventually Melanie and Antonio broke up. Melanie still lives in Aspen, and we see each other frequently, while Don has moved to Santa Barbara, which means that I lost one of my prime golfing buddies. On the other hand, I now have the possibility of working with a third generation of the family. Melanie's daughter, Dakota, has obviously got a lot of talent and consistently makes daring choices.

Dakota, if you need someone to play your grandfather, I'm available.

In 2015, I traveled to Romania to make a movie entitled *What Happened to Monday?* for Raffaella de Laurentiis. My costars were Glenn Close and Willem Dafoe. I had known Glenn only glancingly—we were seated next to each other at a dinner party some years earlier. But even then we discovered mutual interests: Among other things, we had the same drama coach, an amazing man named Harold Guskin. Harold wrote a book entitled *How to Stop Acting*, the gist of which was that acting was about being rather than acting per se. Harold taught in his apartment in New York and inspired great loyalty from his students, among whom were James Gandolfini, Kevin Kline, and Bridget Fonda.

Harold taught you not only to get out of your own way, but also to find out about the other person, which could be defined as the other character, the other actor, or the person you sat next to on the train. For Harold, it wasn't about you, it was about the character—how would the character react, in an honest way, to this situation in which he found himself? Harold and I both believed that the worst thing a director could tell you was how to "act," because you don't want to act, you want to *be*.

Harold had some similarities to Stella Adler, who taught her students how to live as much as she taught them how to act. Stella wanted them to be functioning members of society, to be alive to writing, art, everything that makes up culture. In other words, acting was not something that took place in a vacuum. To be a better actor, you had to be a better person, a better citizen. And beyond that, Harold and Stella both believed that acting was not a matter of producing a reaction in the actor, it was about producing a reaction in the audience. If the actor feels it, but the audience is left cold, what exactly has been accomplished?

Glenn Close

It follows, then, that Glenn is not concerned with stardom or power or any of the ancillary things that accompany fame. She's all about honoring the work. She has some of the same focus and fierceness of Bette Davis and Barbara Stanwyck, and to my mind there is no higher praise for an actress. We thoroughly rehearsed our scenes at our hotel long before we got on the set, and we had several dinners together. She's warm and ingratiating, an interesting woman with a huge amount of professional courage—*Albert Nobbs*, the movie in which she played a Victorian woman who lives her life as a man, was a tour de force that Glenn cowrote. It was just a little ahead of the curve in terms of the public interest in gender fluidity; if it was released today it would attract a lot more of the attention it deserved.

In so many ways, acting is a strange business. You work hard with another actor, and you become entirely open to each other. You give more than the lines; you give them yourself at that moment in time. That kind of emotional openness has to be accompanied by a great deal of trust and mutual respect, so neither of you will be tempted to take advantage of that privileged connection, either professionally or personally. Glenn Close reminds you of what acting, at its best, is all about.

EPILOGUE

Writing this book has forced me to think long and hard about several key questions. One of them is: Do actresses have it harder than actors?

As you may have gathered, I believe the answer is a resounding yes. Now, you may think that insecurity is insecurity, and that it's implicit in the profession, so what's the difference?

Well, let me lay it out for you. It can't be said too often—actresses have shorter careers than actors. This is a generalization, but for every Meryl Streep there are ten Demi Moores and Meg Ryans, women who earned major salaries and major parts for precisely as long as they were the Hot Young Girl and whose professional opportunities began to dry up just about the time they hit forty, or just about the time a fresh crop of hot young girls begin to assert themselves.

This reality is something that every thirty-five-year-old actress knows. When the bell rings signaling another year, and rigorous self-appraisal leads you to the conclusion that you're not Meryl Streep, that bell is not necessarily a cause for celebration, but rather a little ratcheting up of panic.

Is this fair? Hell, no. It's Darwinian. Only the strong—or the hugely talented—survive. That was the case when I came into the business after World War II, and it's the case today.

Men, on the other hand, can and often do go on acting into their fifties and beyond. Occasionally it gets a little uncomfortable. I've mentioned how incongruous it was for Gary Cooper to romance Audrey Hepburn in *Love in the Afternoon*. Honesty compels me to admit that it would have been far less jarring if Cary Grant had taken the part instead, which was indeed offered to him. (Can you believe it? Gary Cooper was second choice!)

The difference was cosmetic; Coop was only three years older than Cary, but he looked fifteen years older. A few years later, Cary and Audrey worked together in *Charade*. Cary was always wary of such an age disparity on-screen, as he was concerned about looking like a dirty old man. He finessed these roles by nudging the writers to make the girl chase him rather than the other way around. Since he was Cary Grant, and was producing most of his later pictures himself, he had a way of getting what he wanted.

But life has no screenwriter, and Cary preferred younger women offscreen. He married Dyan Cannon, had his daughter, Jennifer, with her, and Barbara, his last wife, was decades younger than he was.

A few years ago, I made a movie with Louise Fletcher, who won an Academy Award for her performance in *One Flew Over the Cuckoo's Nest*. I loved her in that movie, but had never met her before we worked together. Louise made the shoot a lovely experience—a fine actress with a great sense of humor, which is crucial for me.

It struck me at the time that Louise's career had suffered because she was simply too good in a completely unsympathetic part. She had played smaller parts before *Cuckoo's Nest*, but that picture was her introduction to a mass audience, and they so completely bought her as Nurse Ratched that the opportunities that followed in the wake of that picture's success were more limited than you would have imagined.

It was the Anthony Perkins problem; Perkins had made many pictures before *Psycho*, but he hadn't seemed to fit into any of them as well as he did as Norman Bates in the Hitchcock picture. The role typed him as a fidgety invert, and it was a type he could never escape.

Tony ultimately did what I had done and went to Europe, where he tried making all sorts of pictures. But he finally capitulated and decided that playing Norman Bates was better than playing nothing at all. He did a batch of sequels to *Psycho* and even directed one of them.

But there was no possibility of sequels to *One Flew Over the Cuckoo's Nest*, so Louise has only rarely had the chance to display her versatility for characters other than control-freak dragon ladies. Believe me, it's the audience's loss.

There's another way that the movies are harder on women: The minute an actress asserts her prerogatives, you can rest assured that there are hundreds of men all too willing to label her a bitch or worse, an attitude that is rarely the response when a male actor makes equivalent demands.

It's not as bad today as it was sixty years ago, but when I got into the movies it was a business run for and by a group of men who expected and appreciated it when women were submissive. When Bette Davis and Olivia de Havilland demanded the same privileges that were granted as a matter of course to male stars—better scripts, more freedom—and would raise holy hell until they got what they wanted, they were granted only a grudging respect.

Modern actresses are generally much more courageous than most of the women I grew up with, but then they can afford to be—they make a lot more money.

In an earlier era, so much energy was spent—or misspent—worrying about the creation of an image and, once that was achieved, its maintenance.

That process resulted in a different kind of actress, one who was beset by constant concerns. Insecurity, mainly. When I was starting out, a lot of actresses—and actors as well—spent a lot of time wondering if they were any good.

But from what I see of young actors today, they don't worry much over what other people might think of their performances. They just go and do them. There's something about this generation that makes them particularly brave; their attitude is, if I fail, I fail. What of it? Onward.

I think the best of the older generation who continue to work are Gena Rowlands and Diane Keaton. Of a younger group, I like Julia Roberts and Helen Hunt. Helen Hunt is a spectacular talent who I suspect is often overlooked because she's not particularly competitive and usually gravitates toward smaller pictures that aren't going to get much attention in a crowded marketplace. But make no mistake—she is the real deal. She and Julia Roberts manage to have it both ways in that they capture both sides of the feminine principle: They can embody a fantasy figure and they can also capture a woman's reality.

And a word needs to be said for Emma Stone and Jennifer Lawrence, both of whom will have long careers.

Someone once asked George Balanchine what would happen to his ballets after he was gone. I like his answer: "People dance while I'm here, they dance a certain way. When I'm gone, they will continue dancing, but somebody will rehearse them different and it will all be a little different, with different approach, different intensity. So a few years go by and I won't be here. Will be my ballets, but will look different."

I like his fatalism in the face of the facts. Things change, and that's the way it has to be. But you'll pardon me if I continue to watch Stanwyck and Davis and Lupino for just a little longer.

All the women in this book had different kinds of careers, different needs as actresses, different needs as women. But almost all of them shared one primary characteristic: They said yes.

They didn't linger on the inequities of show business; they figured that the business had worked to their advantage when they were young, so when the balance of power turned against them when they grew old, that was just the way of the world.

They may have had regrets—we all have those—but very few of them allowed themselves the luxury of bitterness. I don't believe that someone like Irene Dunne missed acting at all, because she had found something to replace it that stimulated her mind and filled her heart. That's the key—not to pine for what was, but to discover what is and what can be.

A great part in a great movie can be transformative for an actor or actress, but there's more to life than that—a yes from a special person. I've been lucky enough to get those. Where would I have been if Minna

Wallis hadn't said yes to a green kid a lifetime ago? For that matter, where would I have been if Barbara Stanwyck hadn't said yes? Or Natalie? Or Jill? My career would have been the same, but my life would have been impoverished.

And when I read a book about Louis B. Mayer and MGM, I said yes to the idea of writing my memoirs with the author of that book, and that has resulted in a third career, one I never expected but have relished. We share the same sense of humor, and Scott knows more about the movie business than most people in the movie business.

So here I am at eighty-six, still adding to the contents of my treasure chest, still working and adding memories—something I hope never changes.

It's the way I am. It's also the way the women I loved in the movies were . . . and are.

ACKNOWLEDGMENTS

I Loved Her in the Movies began with Viking executive editor Rick Kot, who thought the idea would make a great book and proceeded to back up his enthusiasm with a contract and his own encyclopedic knowledge of the movies. It's a cliché to say that real book editors are an extinct species, and it's also inaccurate. Everyone who's lucky enough to work with Rick knows it's not true. Thanks, pal.

Diego Núñez ramrodded the manuscript, the photographs, and the authors with a gentle touch that never failed. And Jason Ramirez came through with a cover design that encapsulates everything sensual and romantic about the movies.

Arranging everything was the amazing Mort Janklow, the literary agent for both authors.

The audio book was recorded at Great Divide Studios in Aspen, Colorado, by Jaimie Rosenberg, director Kevin Thomsen, and producer Sarah Jaffe. Their professionalism sustained even when my voice didn't.

A very special thanks to Jill St. John and Lynn Kalber, our wives, who put up with weeks of cackling laughter cascading from the next room, as we amused ourselves with dueling Cary Grant imitations.

Finally, honesty compels us to thank Max, Mabel, and Clementine, our dogs, who regularly had to postpone their walks because their dads were busy working. They send their very best to Ivy.

INDEX